PRAISE FOR *DAUGHTI*

"Exercising meticulous espionage, Elizabeth Winthrop Alsop gives us a revelatory memoir of the marriage between her famous columnist father and her British mother, who transcribed and interpreted enemy code as a girl. Read *Daughter of Spies* not only for a surprising angle on Vietnam-era Georgetown, but as an acute and heart-wrenching self-portrait of a daughter who insistently loves a difficult mother without breaking her pledge to her own autonomy."

-Honor Moore, author of *Our Revolution, a Mother and Daughter at Midcentury*

"Tish Alsop was a charming, beautiful, well-born war bride of a handsome, dashing, brainy war hero-turned-famous-journalist. They lived together at the center of an elite social group, the 'Georgetown set,' at a time when Washington basically ran the world. But Tish, while brave and stoic, was often lonely and sad and, at times, silently, secretly, desperate. Her daughter, Elizabeth, has written a moving memoir, at once chilling and loving, of her lifelong search for her mother."

-Evan Thomas, author of *The Very Best Men: The Early Years of the CIA*

"A beautifully written, deeply honest memoir. The tales of London during the blitz, and the inside look at the author's family life when her parents lived at the center of power in Cold War Washington are both compelling and revealing. Most of all, Winthrop illuminates her mother's life with poignancy, sympathy and understanding while chronicling with clarity their often complicated relationship."

-Stephen Schlesinger, author of *Bitter Fruit: The Story of the American Coup in Guatemala*

"While deftly evoking the glamour of high society, both in London and in Washington DC, and the tight-lipped secrecy born of war-time espionage—MI 5 and CIA are almost household entities in this family—Elizabeth Winthrop tells how her mother Tish Alsop, having married her American sweetheart at eighteen, had to cope with twelve—twelve!—successive pregnancies and how she struggled with loneliness and addiction, yet maintained her ironic humor to the end. As a daughter, Winthrop is compassionate and clear-eyed; as a writer, she is elegant, even-handed, witty, and incisive, showing that no amount of privilege can protect a woman from misery, and that a stiff upper lip is no solution to pain. The last pages are almost unbearably poignant. Among the chronicles of mother-daughter relationships, this fine memoir gives a fierce lesson in empathy."

-Rosalind Brackenbury, author of *Without Her* and *Becoming George Sand*

"*Daughter of Spies* is a fascinating trip to a country—and a capital—that no longer exists. Part memoir, part elegiac tribute to the author's mother, it is also the story of an extraordinary family that had a powerful influence upon the political and social life of postwar Washington, D.C. In Elizabeth Winthrop Alsop's book, the Georgetown set comes back to life."

-Gregg Herken, author of *The Georgetown Set: Friends and Rivals in Cold War Washington*

"It is an extraordinary challenge for anyone to write a compelling, emotionally honest, personal memoir. To write one in parallel with the public life of a nation that unspools alongside—in this case, much of the 20th-century history of our country—is almost unimaginably difficult. Elizabeth Winthrop Alsop, in *Daughter of Spies*, a recounting of her parents' long marriage as well as her family's prominent role in the affairs of postwar America, has managed this brilliantly, and has done so with perception, wit, humor and enormous compassion. This is the story of a family through the lens of history. Intensely moving, and beautifully done."

-Geoffrey Douglas, author of *Class:The Wreckage of an American Family*

"As a fellow Washingtonian and the offspring of an FBI agent and a CIA librarian, I found that Elizabeth Winthrop Alsop captures perfectly the sinister atmosphere of Cold War Washington. This multilayered memoir takes us on a rich, cinematic journey of great depth and power."

-Tim Gunn author of *Gunn's Golden Rules: Life's Little Lessons for Making it Work*

"This is a fine, tautly controlled memoir of a daughter's wrestling with her ambivalence about her glamorous parents' problems and deceptions. The writer's a child of an English mother who works for MI5 and a dashing yet distant OSS American father who, in World War II, parachutes into France to fight behind the lines with the Resistance. Growing up in a teeming Washington D.C. house filled with a maze of secrets, Elizabeth Winthrop's candid, graceful choreography brings the reader to an inspiring emotional conclusion—it is possible to appreciate, even love our parents' flaws as well as their virtues."

Robert Seidman, author of *Moments Captured*

"Winthrop is a charming writer, and the pages fly by in this profound history of an American family. It starts as a WWII spy story and becomes an intimate portrait of the Washington, D.C. elite in the 1950s and 60s—but throughout it is also an exploration of a relationship with an aging and troubled parent. *Daughter of Spies* is funny, heartbreaking, and beautifully honest."

-Adam Gidwitz, award-winning author of *The Inquisitor's Tale*

"What a superb storyteller Elizabeth Winthrop Alsop is. *Daughter of Spies* is not only a revealing biography of powerful Washington journalist Stewart Alsop and his troubled wife, Tish. It is also a poignant memoir of a daughter emotionally abandoned by her parents. The story—so evocative--will make you both sad and angry, but you'll keep turning pages."

-Douglas Waller, author of *Wild Bill Donovan: The Spymaster who Created the OSS and Modern American Espionage*

DAUGHTER OF SPIES

Wartime Secrets, Family Lies

Elizabeth Winthrop Alsop

Regal House Publishing

Published by
Regal House Publishing, LLC
Raleigh, NC 27587
All rights reserved

ISBN -13 (paperback): 9781646032747
ISBN -13 (epub): 9781646032754
Library of Congress Control Number: 2021949155

All efforts were made to determine the copyright holders and obtain their permissions in any circumstance where copyrighted material was used. The publisher apologizes if any errors were made during this process, or if any omissions occurred. If noted, please contact the publisher and all efforts will be made to incorporate permissions in future editions.

Interior by Lafayette & Greene
Cover design © by C.B. Royal

All images are courtesy of the author unless otherwise specified.

Grateful acknowledgement is made to the following for permission to use copyrighted material:
The photograph on the front cover of the book was taken by Bertram Park, used by permission of Camera Press, London.
The photograph on page 107, used by permission of the Celer and Audax Club of the Kings' Royal Rifle Corp.
The photograph on page 97 was taken by Larry Keighley © SEPS. Licensed by Curtis Licensing, used by their permission. All rights reserved.

Regal House Publishing, LLC
https://regalhousepublishing.com

Printed in the United States of America

For Mummy

INTRODUCTION

My Cell Phone Rings

My cell phone rings often these days. Usually it's Zuni (my mother's live-in Paraguayan housekeeper), or Andrea, who fills in on Zuni's days off. Sometimes it's my mother's secretary Jan, or the geriatric care manager I've hired to oversee the aides I'm bringing into her Washington, DC house. But this time it's my mother herself, a rare occurrence because she can no longer remember phone numbers, or where to find them on the laminated list I've made her, or whether she called me five minutes ago. I answer, as I often do, with my stomach in knots.

Her voice is more imperious than it's been in the last weeks, and her accent still retains a hint of her British colonial childhood. My husband says she sounds like Anthony Hopkins.

"The maid tells me that you no longer want me to drive," she announces, as if this is a little misunderstanding we need to clear up. She's forgotten Zuni's name and that Zuni isn't a maid.

"The doctor doesn't want you to drive."

"Nobody told me that."

"Yes, Mummy, you had an appointment with Dr. S. on the sixteenth and she explained it to you."

"Does that mean I can't even drive myself to mass?"

"That's right."

"Why not?"

"Because you could get faint or dizzy. You could arrive somewhere and not remember how to get home."

"Really?" Now her voice falters. "Well, I do suppose that would be a problem," she admits. "Does this mean I'm never going to be able to drive?"

I take one step back from the truth.

"We'll see." It's what parents say to kids to avoid disappointing them. "The doctor hopes the memory medication will improve things."

Silence. "It's hard," she says at last in a small voice.

"Yes," I acknowledge. "It's very hard."

I am grateful for this moment of parity, a reminder of our most recent relationship, the one we shared for almost thirty years.

At her suggestion, we'd spent a long weekend some years back going over all the aspects of her living will. Did she want to be kept alive if she had a stroke? Should she be hydrated even though hydration would prolong her life? What about pneumonia and antibiotics? The questions we couldn't face were what to do with the stage between independent self-reliance and death, this slow shutting down. That's the stage we're in now, the third stage of our lives together, when sometimes I have to act like her mother and sometimes, she tries to reassert her authority. She relies on me, especially now in her muddled state, to tell her the truth, and I do my best.

"Mummy, I understand you met the nurses yesterday."

"Who are those people? Where did they come from?"

"I've hired them. They give your caregivers someone to call who isn't the doctor or 911. I'm hoping they'll keep you out of the emergency room."

"But I've never been in an emergency room."

"You were there last week, Mummy. For eight hours."

"Oh. I don't remember that."

"Well, that's a day you don't want to remember. Some forgetfulness can be a blessing."

We share a laugh. For a moment she sounds like her old self. And so, I describe it, hoping for a spark of memory.

"Jan was sitting next to you in that emergency room for eight hours. Let's just say that you're going to have to submit to one hour a week of a nurse checking your vitals in order to give me and Jan peace of mind. Not to mention Zuni and Andrea."

"Oh well, if it helps all of you, then I suppose it's fine."

That's always been the way to present something new to my mother. She wants to make it clear that *she* doesn't need anything, but if others do, then she will, of course, oblige. She and my father were distant physically and emotionally from us and from each other, so I had long played "Mum" to my younger brothers. By the time my mother stopped drinking, I was already the mother of my own two children, so I never had to poke through that wall between childhood and adulthood to prove that I belonged on her side of the fence. Perhaps that's why I can speak to her now in a no-nonsense tone of voice that many adult children find it hard to use with their parents when the roles reverse. Or perhaps I'm punishing her. Perhaps both.

Whatever its source, that tough voice is available when I need it. But I'm not enjoying this third stage of our lives together.

"This is hard."

"Yes, Mummy. Very hard."

On both of us.

I want my mother back. If I can't have the one I never had, who was supposed to pick my screaming self out of the crib and hold me close, or cheer at my field hockey game in sixth grade, or attend my college graduation, or teach me how to soothe my own infant daughter, then so be it. I'll settle for the one I had in my middle years, the mother I could phone and talk to for hours about politics, my brothers, my children, the relatives; the mother I took to the Channel Islands to attend her best friend's eightieth birthday; the mother who could remember what her six children were doing and where they lived; the mother who was happier to have me sitting on the couch next to her than anybody else.

It is clear that this new mother, the one who's taken up residence in her body, prefers the dog's company to mine. Morgan, the eleven-year-old corgi, demands nothing of her. He doesn't insist that she track a conversation. He doesn't attempt to discuss the temperature outside or whether the bird on the feeder is a cardinal or a woodpecker. He doesn't turn the radio to her favorite classical station and then look disturbed when she can't figure out how to push the off button on the remote. He doesn't urge her to drink more water or require that she swallow a vanilla protein shake before her third cup of coffee.

He simply settles next to her chair and keeps her company. In the old days, she often chastised him for barking too often or wanting always to be on the other side of the door. Now she talks to him whenever he enters the room, or starts gnawing on one of his toys, or drinks water out of the plant saucers instead of his bowl. At the sound of her voice, he trots over so that her hand, when it drops, comes to rest on his head. That action stills whatever is agitating her. I wish I could live in each moment with her as completely as Morgan does.

My brothers and I are doing all we can to keep her at home, so the trappings remain the same. My mother has always had a certain British upper-class type of beauty, not unlike Queen Elizabeth who was born a month later. The still elegant, silver-haired woman holds court in the garden room from an upholstered, high-backed chair that we call "the throne." We are only partly joking. She is flanked by the jasmine bush she grew from a cutting but can no longer smell, and the huge wooden statue of an eagle from the top of the Los Angeles County courthouse that my father bought on a whim. The laptop computer she now forgets to open rests by her chair; the laminated list I compiled of her friends and family whose names she can't remember, lies next to the phone. The crutches she's had to use for the last fifteen years because of a spinal condition are tucked in easy reach under the coffee table. The bookshelf, filled with books she's read but can no longer follow for even one paragraph, holds photographs of family and a few of the famous people she and my father knew in their Washington heydays. She can't identify most of them.

The person who used to sit in that chair has slipped out the back door. She went quietly. We didn't heed the warning signs, although recognizing them wouldn't have made a difference. We just kept hoping, as so many adult children do, that she would be able to live as full a life as possible and die in her sleep.

&

My mother's life falls into three parts. The first lasts from her birth in 1926, in Gibraltar, until her marriage to my father at the age of eighteen. The second covers the years of marriage and childbearing until she became a widow at forty-eight. The third and longest stage is life on her own, now thirty-five years and still counting. In many ways, quiet independence has suited her personality. In our large, boisterous family, she was always reserved, a person we children didn't know very well. When my brothers and I were growing up in post-war Washington, my American father's family dominated our lives.

My father's family lived up and down the East Coast, and we spent every Christmas and part of every summer with our Alsop grandmother and cousins on a shade tobacco and dairy farm in Avon, Connecticut. We knew the names of the cows in the barn. We knew Emma the cook, who slipped us spoonfuls of cookie dough from the pale brown crockery mixing bowl pressed against her uniformed bosom. We knew Aggie Guthrie, the Scottish girl who arrived at the farm in 1911 to raise my father and his three siblings. On every visit, we tiptoed back into the dark corner of Grandmother's living room to stare with ghoulish wonder at the mummy's hand, a disintegrating relic inside a glass case that some Alsop or Roosevelt ancestor had stolen from an Egyptian tomb.

My paternal grandmother was Theodore Roosevelt's niece, the only daughter born to his younger sister, Corinne. My grandmother's closest female first cousins were Alice Roosevelt Longworth—Theodore's eldest daughter, who lived near us in Washington—and Eleanor Roosevelt. Eleanor had defected from the Theodore side of the family into which she was born, when she married that "feather duster," Franklin, so even though she and my grandmother remained friends through family spats and political divisions, nobody thought it was important that any of us be introduced to FDR's widow. (She died when I was fourteen.) The Roosevelt name lingered in the family shadows, but we weren't brought up to dwell on it or use it to further any cause. We did, however, have an enormous allegiance to the very American Alsop tribe.

The only one of my mother's relatives that we knew was her mother, Cecilia—Granny we called her—who came from her home in Gibraltar every September, right around my birthday, and stayed for three months while my father traveled abroad reporting and writing weekly columns for the *Herald Tribune* newspaper syndicate. Granny seemed impossibly old-fashioned and prissy in an English nanny sort of way, with a patina of Latin exoticism. She wore a black lace mantilla to daily mass. Like my mother, she spoke a kind of kitchen Spanish to the maids or anyone who looked vaguely Latin. She insisted on cleaning the bookshelves one book at a time, implying the inadequacy of my mother's housekeeping. For the one or two days when their paths crossed, she and my father would renew their longstanding battle over the ashes in the fireplace. She thought they should be removed; he liked them to build up over a winter to ensure a hotter flame. She seemed rigid and opinionated. I sensed that, like us, my mother endured these visits more than she enjoyed them. We knew nothing of Granny's life and with the casual cruelty of self-absorbed children, we didn't care. We didn't like to be told to polish our shoes, sit up at the table, and mind our manners. During Granny's visits, we skulked around, avoided her as much as possible and waited for our father's return, as it signaled Granny's departure.

It wasn't until I was well into my fifties and my father had been dead for over twenty years that I began to ask my mother about her life. The stories that came spilling out of her, rich with detail and emotions, felt as if they had been dammed up for years in the deep pool of her memory.

"Nobody ever asked about my childhood," my mother said to me when I began to interview her on tape. "They didn't want to know what I'd been through before I got here." As a child, it didn't occur to me to wonder about her grandparents, or whether she had a pet, or what house she grew up in. The names Gibraltar, Algeciras, Kent, and Fetcham cropped up occasionally in her conversations, but the places seemed far away and foreign to our American ears.

And then there were the boxes, shipped long ago from

Gibraltar, shoved in the basement, and forgotten. They are a treasure trove now.

I think people are either editors or pack rats. I'm an editor. Living in a New York apartment is a bit like living in a boat. My rule is, "Nothing comes in, but that something must go out." My mother's a pack rat. Except for the years during the war when she stayed in her parents' two-bedroom flat in London, my mother has always lived in large houses. So, when it became time to help her "downsize" from the eleven-bedroom house in Washington where we all grew up to a four-bedroom house a few miles away, I was prepared for the job of cataloging the antique furniture, the china, and the paintings that had passed down through generations on both sides of my family. What came as a complete shock were the boxes of memorabilia we found tucked away in the basement, much of it from my mother's family, the Hankeys. Eighteenth-century deeds and certificates noting births, marriages, deaths from England and Gibraltar were all jumbled together with letters from her brother, Ian, and photograph albums from their childhood.

"Mummy, where did all this come from?" I asked as I labeled the boxes for the move to the new basement.

"Back in the early 1970s, when I had to move your grandmother from Gibraltar to that nursing home in England, I had it all crated up and shipped to me here. Your father was sick at the time, so I didn't have a chance to sort through any of it." She smiled wearily. "I guess I never got around to it."

Now, as she slips deeper into dementia, those basement boxes provide hours of entertainment and give us a way back to each other. Sitting on the sofa next to her chair, I ask her to read to me from the parchment documents so I can catalogue them. For a moment, she is not muddled or confused, does not protest that something's gone wrong with her eyes. The high-flown language is familiar to her, and she dials up the British accent just a little. One of our favorites is the official commissioning of her uncle Wilfred as a Second Lieutenant in the Land Forces. Dated 1902, it begins: *Edward by the Grace of God of the United Kingdom of Great Britain and Ireland and of the British Dominions beyond the Seas, King, Defender of the Faith, Emperor of India, Etc. To our Trusty and well-beloved Wilfred Humphrey Mosley, Gentleman, Greeting.* And so on and so forth. We giggle together over the language, the lofty tone, the elaborate stamps and signatures.

I wish I could give us more times like these.

In the last few years, my mother has been telling people that I'm writing her autobiography. I don't bother to correct her. It isn't an autobiography, because, of course, she's not writing it. It's not even a biography, because it's also featuring me. I've been researching her life because I want to get down her story before she leaves us, but also because it helps pass the interminable hours when our only topics of conversation have become the birds on the feeder and whether the dog has gone out. I need to figure out how she got to be the mother she was, but at the same time, I'm trying to hang on to her as she slips away. *Stay here with me, Mummy. Read to me. Tell me more stories.*

Before I even thought of writing this book, I knew I wanted to get every story out of her while she could still tell them, so I'd have no regrets when she was gone. Friends who'd lost their own mothers had warned me about that. Ask her now, they said, before she dies. Stupidly, it never occurred to me that she could leave me without dying. This way. By inches. Asking her about dates or meetings or moments in her long ago past has now begun to feel cruel, as if I'm poking at an open wound. I keep promising myself that I will slow down and learn to live with her in the moment, but the researcher in me often forgets.

I'm looking for answers. Who were you, you two strangers who became my parents? What drew you to each other? Did the love survive the marriage? And then the harder ones. Why were you such an absent mother, especially for me, the only girl in the house? Was it your natural British reserve that made you hold yourself apart? Or were you trying to shield your children from your own deep despair soothed only by the vodka stirred into your Coca-Cola?

Maybe I think the writing of this book will crack the barrier, get near the coded self that she withheld from everyone. Maybe it will help me to age differently, so that at the end, I won't be as alone and sad and isolated as she is.

Maybe I'm just kidding myself.

"Old age is a shipwreck," my uncle used to say. So right he was.

PART I

My Parents' Love Affair

My Mother's Childhood
Gibraltar
1926–1939

Gib is short for Gibraltar, a rocky peninsula attached to the southern coast of Spain that was claimed by a British Admiral in 1704 on his way back from a failed attempt to capture Barcelona. In 1713, the territory was ceded in perpetuity to Great Britain under the Treaty of Utrecht, and the Spanish have been trying to reclaim it ever since. Gibraltarians have repeatedly voted against proposals for Spanish sovereignty, preferring to remain a British Overseas Territory, what used to be called a Crown Colony.

Born on St. Patrick's Day in 1926, my mother was named Patricia, but was always known as Tish. Unlike me, she had only one brother, Ian, who was sent to boarding school in England when she was three and killed in the war when she was sixteen. She might as well have been an only child.

Gibraltarians call themselves mongrels because the settlers came from every one of the countries that ring the Mediterranean, as well as from Britain. My mother's father, Arthur Hankey, was a shipping merchant, brought up in Surrey, England, while his wife's ancestors emigrated from Spain, England, Ireland, and Italy. The family lived in a Georgian house on Prince Edward's Road, directly across the street from Hargrave's Parade where the army drilled its troops. In the afternoons, whenever the band struck up, the neighborhood children poured out of their houses to march up and down in time with the soldiers, cursing at one another in imitation of the sergeant swearing at his men.

The marble entrance to the yellow house was freezing cold

in the winter as it sat directly under a huge tank which collected water during the rainy season, November through March. Upstairs, on the balcony that connected the elegant drawing room and a formal dining room, Polynesia, Ian's parrot, perched on the wrought-iron balustrade and imitated the street vendors. "*Verduras frescas*," he would call out in a loud voice, cackling as the people further up the lane popped their heads out of windows ready to buy vegetables.

Besides the cook, a housemaid, and a parlor maid who lived in during the week, the laundress came Monday to Friday from across the border in Spain. In the laundry room on the top floor of the house, she washed the clothes in water heated over a charcoal stove and then hung them up on long lines strung out above the flat roof. The flapping garments tempted the Barbary apes down from their preserve at the top of the Rock, as they loved to dress themselves in whatever they managed to snatch off the line. The laundress was terrified of the apes who bit. When the household down below heard the shrieking, it was my mother, always good in a crisis, who rushed up to the roof with a broom to frighten off the animals.

My mother was born in a time and place where one war was just a warm-up for the next.

From the flat roof of the Hankey house there was a 360-degree view: north over the cemetery to the border town of La Linea, west for the sunsets over Algeciras, south to the mountains of Morocco and Ceuta, and east directly into the sheer gray wall of rock that rose up behind the house.

One evening in mid-July of 1936, when my mother was ten years old, she heard the sound of guns and screaming. Her parents had gone out for dinner, but she and the maids and Jill, the terrier, all climbed up to the roof to see what was going on.

Fires were burning all over La Linea, and the constant pop of guns in the distance sounded like firecrackers. As the maids watched the clouds of smoke rising over their own homes, they began to shriek and cling to one another. It was their reaction more than the battle noise that terrified my mother, who slipped downstairs to her bedroom, where she and Jill curled up together under the covers and waited for her parents to come home. They'd witnessed one of the first battles of the Spanish Civil War.

Some weeks later, the family was crossing to Campamento in Spain for Sunday lunch with Tish's grandmother, Mercedes, when the car was stopped by a border guard. They were first in line, and Tish had been allowed to sit in the front of the Vauxhall next to her father. Perched on the edge of her seat with her window slid down, she could see the feluccas, the gaff-rigged fishing boats with dark red sails, pulled up on the shore. On this day they were carrying soldiers. A long line of Moors, armed with antique rifles slung across their Bedouin robes, marched off the boats and up the hill toward the Hankey's car. The citizens of La Linea had come down to the water to watch, but nobody spoke. The soldiers' sandals hit the cobblestones with a rhythmic slap, slap, slap. Here were the Moors, the people who'd ruled this country for seven centuries, brought back to Spanish soil by Francisco Franco. It didn't take long for the four or five platoons to pass. The soldiers disappeared over the crest of the hill, the guard blew his whistle, and the crowd began to disperse. There was no sense of violence, just shock and the fear of what was to come.

But the Hankeys lived at the edge of this war. Although the early battles began in Andalucia, the fighting moved gradually north, and the British in Gibraltar resumed their daily lives— riding to hounds at the annual point-to-point race, shopping on Saturdays in the center of town, in what was known as the Jews Market, playing bridge in the British Ladies' Club, and traveling home to England for the summer holidays.

Once her older brother left for boarding school, my mother might as well have been an only child. As army and navy personnel were never stationed on the Rock for more than a year or two, it was hard for her to form any lasting friendships with their children. So it was not surprising that at the age of thirteen, she begged to go away to school herself. Her parents chose Poles, a convent school in Ware, north of London, the only place they considered high enough quality for a British girl raised Catholic. Ampleforth, the school her brother attended in Yorkshire, was designated the Eton for Catholic boys, and Poles had the same reputation for girls.

Poles Convent, Ware, England

My grandparents' timing was odd. They sent their teenage daughter away in April, the middle of spring term, when the other students had already formed their friendships. Luckily, another girl, also named Patricia but called Bee, arrived at the same awkward moment in the semester. The two Patricias bonded instantly, and the friendship lasted through war and a lifelong transatlantic separation until Bee's death at the age of eighty-two.

The spring of 1939 was an unsettled time to start anything. That summer, Arthur's mother, known as Granny Hankey, rented a grouse moor at Berwick on Tweed just over the border on the Northumberland coast. The Tom Hankey cousins from their tea plantation in Ceylon, the four Arthur Hankeys from Gib, Aunt Miriam and her companion, Ann, and their dogs, and other assorted cousins and retainers boarded the Flying Scotsman at Cheltenham in Gloucestershire for the trip north.

This grouse moor was considered "second class" compared

to the ones Granny Hankey usually rented in the Scottish Highlands. The main house was lit by gas lamps that had to be trimmed every day. The ghillie (Scottish word for gamekeeper) had no staff, so the shooters and the children acted as beaters, walking out into the grass in a single line with sticks to flush the game.

They were all paying special attention to the war news as Tish's father would have to return to Gibraltar immediately if war was declared. September 3, the day that Neville Chamberlain was scheduled to speak to the nation, my mother, her brother, and her parents all trooped down to the ghillie's cottage as he was the only one with electricity and a radio. It had been raining for days and the dogs lay sprawled on the stone floor; forever after, my mother connected England's declaration of war with the smell of damp spaniel.

Back she went to Poles, where the nuns of the order of the Faithful Companions of Jesus ("Bee and I called them the Frightful Chums," my mother once told me) maintained radio silence and forbade any discussion of war or outside events. Although she'd only been at school since the spring term, my mother was beginning to wonder why she'd begged to leave her cosseted life on the Rock. The unheated convent buildings remained drafty all year round, the nuns were strict and humorless, and Tish felt so cut off that the world outside might as well not have existed.

After the declaration of war, Britain prepared by handing out gas masks and evacuating children from the cities to the country, but for a long time nothing happened. During Christmas that year—a year which came to be known as the "Phony War"—the Hankey family reconvened at Aunt Ida and Uncle Hugh's house in Gloucestershire for the holidays. It was so cold that for the first time in years, the huge lake in front of Eastnor Castle froze all the way across. Tish's cousins, Peter and Roger, gave her skating lessons while Ian, now used to Yorkshire winters from his years at Ampleforth boarding school, turned circles around them, urging her on. The three boys escorted Tish to her first proper dance, an aristocratic coming-out party for the daughter of the sixth Baron Somers at Eastnor, their family seat. At thirteen, Tish was far too young for this kind of thing, but Aunt Ida called the debutante's mother who said, "Of course, why not? The whole world is about to be turned upside down. Why not let the girl have some fun?"

The four drove off in an ancient car with Peter at the wheel. Tish floated into the room surrounded by her handsome squires, who danced with her and bribed their friends to do the same. Some nameless young man took her in to dinner and, although she said barely a word and was too excited to eat, it remained one of the most memorable nights of her life.

After that Christmas in December of 1939, the family split up again, the parents heading back to Gibraltar and the two children to their respective schools. On their way north to Yorkshire, Ian, Roger, and Peter stopped off in Birmingham so that Ian and Peter, who'd both recently turned eighteen, could enlist. They didn't tell their parents.

My mother has always been undemanding when it comes to holidays. She's perfectly happy to have Christmas dinner with friends and urges the six of us children to celebrate at home with our own families. Maybe she was forced to drag us children up to our Connecticut grandparents one too many times. This arrangement also gets her out of the tree decorating and stocking stuffing, chores she always resented because they fell so squarely on her shoulders. My father considered anything to do with the children and the household entirely a woman's job. But now, as her world grows smaller and her friends begin to age and die, I feel guilty about leaving her with Zuni and an afternoon visit from Jan, even though I know that a holiday for her might be no different than any other day.

I decide we should spend Thanksgiving with her, but it's not long before I begin to feel trapped. The time drags because there are so few topics of conversation that sustain us. The pain in her back comes and goes, but she's grown edgier and more impatient since my last visit. So much of the last fifteen years of her life has been about living with pain. It's hard to watch her struggle to walk from the garden room back to her bathroom or out to the car, planting each crutch, one at a time, in front of her. She won't give up. I'm reminded of something a friend said about her own mother, who contracted a staph infection in the hospital at eighty-eight and lived for four more miserable months. Why does she keep fighting?

Her stories are now completely unreliable. She gets dates, times, and names wrong, but is so insistent on her facts that nobody argues with her. Friends come for Thanksgiving dinner, and Zuni and I do the cooking, while my husband sits with my mother in the garden room and listens to her tell the same story two or three times in an hour. It's as if her brain gets stuck in a loop and can't unstick itself.

Confused by the crowd of people sitting around her dining room, she looks out at us from what feels like an increasingly distant island, floating away inch by inch to another horizon. She knows that she knows somebody but can't necessarily summon up the name. She covers by shrinking into herself, speaking less and less, and we cover by babbling across her. In my childhood, her alcoholism was the elephant in the room. Now it's her dementia.

Ironically, for a woman who married into a large, noisy family and who had six children, my mother remained an introvert, more comfortable sharing a cup of tea with one person than staring at a crowd of faces around the dinner table. I realize too late that I should have left her alone with Zuni for this holiday too, safely inside her bubble.

For a brief period, that second third of her life, the bubble included me. No longer. It enrages me to find myself, once again, in that all too familiar role as the wary watcher on the outside looking in.

THE WAR COMES

1940–1942

In the spring of 1940, with very little warning, my grandmother Cecilia showed up at Poles and told my mother to pack her bags. She'd decided to take her two children home to Gibraltar. She was worried that her son would enlist (unbeknownst to her, he already had) and that her daughter was too close to London, the first place the Germans were sure to bomb. She handed my mother her very first passport, which had been issued back in Gibraltar just days before her March birthday.

The official document notes that Patricia Barnard Hankey is

Tish's 1940 passport photo taken when she was thirteen

five-foot, five-inches tall, has light brown hair and brown eyes. In the small square photograph, she's dressed in a loose-fitting overcoat with wide open lapels, and a black-and-white striped shirt that looks like something a dancer, cast as a sailor, might have worn in a vaudeville show. Her hair, parted in the very middle of her forehead, has been stretched tight across the top of her skull to pigtails anchored by black grosgrain bows. The freckles sprinkled over the bridge of her nose do nothing to belie her wary stare. Her brown eyes are alert, unflinching, her expression solemn and bright. Despite the pigtails, she looks older than her years.

᪐

Usually, the Hankeys traveled to and from England through the

Bay of Biscay, a crossing my mother dreaded as the famously rough waters always made her seasick. But this time, Cecilia decided to give them a little treat by taking the ferry from Folkestone to Calais, and then the train to Paris. They stayed at a pension but skipped the Louvre which had been emptied of important paintings on the day war was declared. During a production of *Carmen* at the Paris Opera, even dour Cecilia had to smile when her two children got a fit of giggles over the lead tenor, whose tights split in the middle of an aria. On April 13, they landed in Gibraltar, just days after Hitler invaded Denmark and Norway.

My mother was thrilled to be home on this unexpected vacation from dank British weather and dreary war news. Romulus and Remus, her beloved corgis, greeted her with abandon. The oleander was blooming, the sun shone warm, and everything on the Rock felt familiar and safe. But their sojourn was to be short-lived.

In mid-May, the Nazis moved into France, Belgium, and the Netherlands. On the fifteenth, Holland surrendered. On the twentieth, the Governor General of Gibraltar issued the official evacuation order, stating that all women and children were to leave the Rock within three days. While the Spanish Civil War had little immediate impact on the Hankey family, even my fourteen-year-old mother sensed that this new war would change everything. The losses began right away, on May 23, the day she, her brother, and mother boarded their evacuation ship, the SS *Ormonde,* bound for Southampton Harbor.

While my mother and my grandmother stood side by side on the deck watching their household possessions swing in a rope net over the open water, the hawser suddenly gave way. One trunk and two of my mother's three precious boxes of books slid into the sea. There was no time to salvage the loss. The crew loaded up the next rope sling. The trunk held family linen, passed down through generations. Cecilia tightened her grip on the handrail but didn't say a word. My mother knew not to complain. What were a few books against everything else they'd had to leave behind? Far more devastating losses were to come.

Setting out, the ship followed another filled with Gibraltar evacuees, zigzagging across the Atlantic in an effort to dodge the U-boats. Three days later, when the passengers thronged to the rail for their first sight of Southampton Harbor, the announcement came that they were being held so that mine sweepers could clear the harbor. In a process known as degaussing, the hull of their ship, like the others, had been wiped with an electrical cable to demagnetize the metal, and repel the mines dropped the night before by German submarines. They waited with engines throbbing until the all-clear sounded in the distance, followed some minutes later by an enormous explosion. Slowly, without any further announcement from the bridge, the *Ormonde* backed away. The ship from Gibraltar they'd been following for the last three days had blown up. The sweepers had missed a mine and the degaussing had failed.

They sailed up the English Channel, hugging the coast so closely that my mother could pick out the red double-decker buses going up the Folkestone Road. The channel was crowded with boats even as, in France, the guns thundered away. Every few minutes, a large ship crossed their bow. The captain had been ordered to maintain radio silence, so the passengers had no idea they were witnessing the first day of the evacuation of the British Expeditionary Force from Dunkirk.

Horns and whistles blew. Like great whales, the barrage balloons tethered to buoys floated overhead to keep the Germans from attacking both the shipping lanes and the evacuation boats. A convoy of fifty empty tankers, high in ballast, gave way to troop ships crossing their bow.

Tish and Ian, old hands at making this trip, called the other children on deck for their favorite game. The seagulls hovered just above the children's heads. The first one in line held up a piece of breakfast toast and down dipped a gull to snatch it and wheel away. Tish set up the next child, Ian handed out the toast, and the game was repeated again and again. If a gull tried to jump the queue, the others attacked until it fell back. If a child tried to jump the queue, the same thing happened. The mothers on board were grateful. The game passed the time and distracted the younger ones from the boom of guns across the water. When the boat docked up the Thames at Tilbury Port, Cecilia wasted no time in getting her daughter to Liverpool station for the train to Ware. Before my mother had a moment to take stock, she was back behind the walls of Poles convent, news of the war now muffled by the smothering nuns.

The day they landed, Ian finally admitted to his mother that he'd enlisted back in January. After a week with Cecilia in a small London hotel, he boarded a train at Paddington to join his officer cadet training unit at Norton Barracks near Worcester. A few weeks later, Cecilia took the top flat at 60 Pont Street in central London where her sister and brother were already living with their families.

Tish didn't see Gibraltar again for nine years.

I started taping my mother's memories years before her slide into dementia, and the stories often start the same way. For example, about that journey up the English Channel on the first day of Dunkirk, she always begins, "Anybody who was there will tell you, it was a bluebird day." But often when I'm hearing the story for the third or fourth time, she'll add a detail, or I'll think of another question. One spring day, when I've convinced her to sit out in the garden, I remember about all the Hankey family pets. What happened to them? I ask.

"Sometime that summer, my father gave Polynesia the parrot to the butler at Government House. She was killed by flying glass during one of the bombing raids by the Vichy Air Force. As far as I know, she was the only casualty."

"How sad."

"It was for the best, really. What would we have done with her?" I am often startled by my mother's lack of feeling, but I keep my voice steady when I ask the next question. If she's not showing any emotion, then I had better not either. Cecilia, Tish, me. We learn early on how to grip the handrail without speaking.

"And your corgis? Romulus and Remus?"

"During the war, there was a ban on pets coming into England. In September of 1940, when my father was forced to leave Gibraltar along with all the non-military civilians, he tried to sneak the dogs into England. What a hopeless idea." As a child she'd adored her father, but when she mentions him now, because of their post-war history, her tone is often dismissive. "Daddy got them on the evacuation ship, but they were discovered by the British quarantine officer at Tilbury Port."

Silence.

"So, what happened?"

"They were shot and buried at sea."

I hope Grandfather didn't have to shoot them himself. I hope he didn't have to watch. But I don't speak these thoughts. I hold still and wait, knowing she will bristle at any sign of emotion over pets killed almost seventy years ago.

"We barely had enough food for humans," she says into the silence. "We could never have fed two dogs."

Later, I ask what she remembers of the years between May 1940, when she was evacuated, and August 1942, when she met Daddy. Five years ago, she could have answered the question easily. Now, anything to do with dates completely confuses her, but I try anyway.

"You said once that your mother took you to Liverpool Station and put you on a train to school." I am speaking slowly and distinctly. "You came off the ship in Tilbury Port, and two hours later you were back at Poles."

"What ship was that?"

"It was called the SS *Ormonde*, the one that evacuated you and Granny and Uncle Ian out of Gibraltar."

There is a pause as she tries to absorb all these details. I realize I've given her too many names and dates at once.

"Well, I suppose my mother was desperate to get me out of London," she remarks. "When was that again?"

"May 28, 1940."

Another silence.

"Well, dear, how are you?" she asks at last. She's forgotten already what we are talking about. This has become her stock question, the one she uses to move the conversation along. Recently, she told me that she doesn't call people on the phone anymore because she doesn't know what to say to them.

I will leave in the morning without saying goodbye, because she'll be focused on dressing for the trainer who comes twice a week. When you are dependent on crutches, every move you make must be carefully planned. She allows the trainer to give her a ten-minute massage at the end of their exercise session, and I'm glad she experiences physical touch from someone.

I don't remember my mother or father ever hugging me. This lack is beginning to break my heart, not for me but for her. My children and a loving husband have taught me to give and accept hugs, but she's never moved beyond the undemonstrative reserve learned the hard way in childhood.

My Parents Meet

Even though my parents had a wildly romantic love affair in England during the war, they were woefully mismatched. Tish was young, British, Catholic, and undereducated, yet too experienced for her age. My father, Stewart, was twelve years older, a naïve American, irreligious, and a Yale graduate.

In September of 1931, when she was five and sailing with her family on the SS *Rajputana* from Gibraltar to London to take her older brother back to school in Yorkshire, my father was starting his final year at his boarding school in New England. When, at ten, she watched the first battle of the Spanish Civil War from her parents' roof in Gibraltar, he had just been suspended from Yale for removing all the hubcaps from a policeman's car. When he landed his first job in New York after college, she was ten years old, attending the Brympton School in Gibraltar. In April of 1942, after he'd been turned down repeatedly by the American armed forces because of high blood pressure and asthma, he managed to enlist in a British regiment and landed in England, just as she was eagerly counting down the days to graduation from Poles. The late summer night when they were seated next to each other at dinner, he was a cossetted and immature twenty-eight-year-old, while she was sixteen and wise beyond her years.

In August of that year, two months after her graduation from Poles, my mother was winding up another summer with her friend Bee at Allerton Park, the Premier Baron Mowbray's gloomy baronial castle in northern Yorkshire. The two girls were enrolled at Carr Saunders Secretarial School starting in September so they could be trained for war work.

Allerton Park, Knaresborough, England

Bee's father, William Marmaduke Stourton, the twenty-fifth Baron Mowbray, was a terrifying character with white-blond hair and a sudden, explosive temper. (The Premier Baron of England is usually Catholic, and the Baron Mowbray title was created by writ in 1283.) He was married to Sheila Gulley, a granddaughter of the First Viscount Selby, who served as speaker of the House of Commons from 1895 to 1905. She was pretty, distant, and emotionally fragile.

Upon learning that the castle was to be requisitioned by the Royal Canadian Air Force for the duration of the war, Lord and Lady Mowbray decided to throw one last wild party before moving into a cottage on the estate. My father and his friend George Thomson, both Americans training with the Kings Royal Rifle Corps in York, were invited to the party by one Lieutenant Whitehead, a cousin of Lady Mowbray's.

The three men approached the front door where, they hammered and hallooed and rang the bell for quite some time, but all in vain. Nothing happened. Whitehead had forgotten they were supposed to go around by the side door since there was no longer any staff to hover by the formal entrance. For this party, the Mowbrays were making do with an ancient butler and a cook with a wooden leg. In the drawing room, someone finally heard the bell, and Lord Mowbray himself agreed to go answer it as the butler was still creaking around the room balancing a tray with the first round of drinks on his trembling left arm. Lord Mowbray snatched his own martini from the tray and stumped off down the hallway with his daughter Bee and her friend Tish trailing along behind.

My mother's first sight of the man she would marry was of a ghostly face hovering in the middle of a circle he'd wiped in the grimy side windowpane with his handkerchief. He winked at her. Then his face disappeared and was replaced by White-head's.

"Who the devil is that?" thundered Lord Mowbray, who'd already tossed off his martini in one gulp.

"It's St. John Whitehead," my mother said as Lord Mowbray hauled open the enormous wooden door. In the feeble light from the hall, the three inside could just make out the three soldiers in uniform huddled together on the front steps.

"Lord Mowbray, good to see you," gushed Whitehead. When the baron paid no attention to his outstretched hand, the lieutenant mumbled introductions and slipped past him, headed for the drawing room.

The two Yanks looked uncertainly at Lord Mowbray. Tish and Bee waited to see what would happen next.

"Are you Americans?" demanded Lord Mowbray, his blue eyes bulging.

George Thomson admitted that yes, regretfully, they were.

"Good God," said Lord Mowbray. "Always had a rule here, back to my grandfather's time. No motor cars. No Americans."

Everybody froze while he considered this ancient tradition.

Finally, he shrugged and motioned to them to follow. "Well, you're here. You might as well come in." And so they all fell into line and followed him into the sitting room, where the party was already in full swing.

At dinner, my mother told my father that he looked like a criminal because of his military haircut. He was enchanted. She didn't babble and chatter like a Long Island debutante. In fact, he couldn't get another word out of her all through dinner. Two years of living with rations had taught her to focus on the food while he sampled the wines from the baron's excellent cellar. At one thirty a.m., urged on by several glasses of port, he kissed her in a dark corner of the rose garden and immediately proposed marriage.

In a letter home the next week, he admitted that even in the cold light of day, and even though he often proposed to young women when he'd had too much to drink, this time he thought it was a pretty good idea as she was a real charmer and the daughter of a belted earl. This last proved not to be true, but he was often prone to exaggeration when it came to describing his latest love interest. His parents were amused, as they usually were, by Stewart's antics. Lady Mowbray was horrified when Lord Mowbray reported to her that Tish had been found kissing an *American* in the rose garden. (He didn't admit that he'd been standing in another corner with his arms wrapped around his own mistress.) Lady Mowbray immediately wrote to Cecilia, advising that she needed to take Tish in hand immediately in order to "curb her hot Spanish blood."

Tish didn't pay much attention to any of it. In wartime, anything could happen, and the American soldier was so much older and in training at the other end of England from her secretarial school. Flattered as she was by this handsome man's attentions, she couldn't imagine she'd ever see him again.

In my mother's childhood photograph albums, there's a picture of the four members of the Hankey family—Tish, Ian, and their parents—in the garden of Vista Allegre, which was their last house in Gibraltar, the one they were evacuated from with three days' notice in May of 1940. This photo was taken in 1938. The four are standing in a solemn row, Ian looking as if he's just skidded into place in the line. He's trying out the self-timer on his brand-new camera. Once he's set it carefully on the wall, peered through the viewfinder, ordered his family to move this way or that, and finally released the timed shutter, he has to run to get into the picture. My grandmother looks peevish, my grandfather stiff, and my mother, a sulky ten-year-old, has her arms crossed impatiently. One can almost hear her foot tapping.

It's the last picture of them all together.

The Hankey Family at Vista Allegre, Gibraltar

My grandmother didn't answer Lady's Mowbray's letter about Tish's inappropriate behavior because by the time it arrived, a telegram had come in from the war office with the news that on August 31, 1942, twenty-year-old Ian Barnard Hankey had been killed in the battle of Alam Halfa in the Western Desert. Divebombed by a Stuka, he'd taken out two German tanks himself before he died. In the condolence letter that reached his family six weeks later, his commanding officer reported that Ian *was killed instantly and can have known no pain.* My grandparents decided that he should be buried with his comrades in a British military cemetery in Egypt.

Although she didn't know it then, the same day that her childhood ended with the death of her brother, the door to Tish's future slid open when she was seated next to the American subaltern, training in York with the Kings Royal Rifle Corps.

❧

I am my father's daughter. Even though I've made my living writing fiction, I've always loved the research, the journalistic hunt for the correct detail.

One day when I walk into the garden room, my mother leans over to retrieve a large white manila envelope from under her chair. "These are your uncle Ian's papers. Do you want to take a look at them? I really don't have the energy to go through it all myself."

"Where did you find these?" I ask.

"They were down in the cellar with those other things we moved from the old house. Someone brought a box upstairs," she says. "I can't remember who. I get so muddled these days."

I make an excuse to disappear to my bedroom and tuck the envelope in my suitcase before she can change her mind. Sometimes she doesn't want me to take things out of the house. She's scared of losing the bits and pieces of her history. Who can blame her? So much was scattered to the winds by the war, the evacuations, her emigration to America. And now her mind is slipping away. She is pleased I'm recording it all as fast as I can, as she's the last one left who can tell her story.

For a while I become obsessed with my uncle Ian. I spend hours reading through his school reports and retyping the war letters written in between the battles in Libya and Egypt, and then later, the letters of condolence to his parents.

I do better with my mother on the phone than when we rub up against the dailiness of each other. This is a book she will never see, but I read her sections from time to time. When I try to weave Ian's story into hers and expand on what she's given me with details based on my research, she gets irritated.

Yesterday she said, "Well, don't ask me for all the facts if you're not going to get them straight."

And I shot back, "They are right, Mummy. I checked my sources."

Immediately, I want to suck the words back into my mouth. How unkind I am to be arguing with my eighty-two-year-old mother who's desperately trying to hold on to her independence and her memories.

I am first and foremost a fiction writer, so I keep trying to shape the facts of her life to fit my vision. I'm also probably trying to reshape my mother. She gets most irritated when I assign her some emotion she long ago repressed or no longer remembers.

"Weren't you sad when Ian was sent off to school?"

"All the boys went at that age. You have to remember he was four and a half years older than me. When you're a child, that's an eternity. We were never very close," she adds dismissively.

It reminds me of her attitude toward Romulus and Remus, or Polynesia the parrot, killed by flying glass. It happened a long time ago, and there was nothing to be done about it. After a lifetime of practice hiding feelings deemed inconvenient or in-appropriate, she is now a master.

She does have a few specific memories of her brother during the war. There was the time she and Bee joined him in the flat at 60 Pont Street for the May 1941 weekend that turned out to be the last bad night of the Blitz. The Hankey parents had gone fishing in Scotland, so the three teenagers teamed up with others in the neighborhood in a vain attempt to put out the fire engulfing St. Columba's church across the street. All the fire engines were down in the East End, fighting to save the docks, so by morning, nothing was left of the church but four blackened walls.

And there was the time Ian came to Poles to take the two girls out to lunch. A handsome, dark-haired nineteen-year-old in full dress uniform, he attracted lots of attention. Bee and Tish were the envy of the other students who hung out the windows, waving and hallooing.

"He'd managed to get his hands on a car, but unfortunately it didn't have any brakes so we spent our time running the front wheels into the grass so we could slow down on the long slope into town."

"That was the last time you saw him?"

"Yes. He shipped out to North Africa in August of 1941 and was killed exactly a year later. On August 31. The day I met your father."

My Father's Life

1914–1942

My father was born in Avon, Connecticut, in 1914, the third child and second son of an odd couple. Joseph Wright Alsop IV was a shade tobacco and dairy farmer from a Middletown, Connecticut family who traced their lineage back to sixteenth century English pub owners—hence the name Alsop which comes from the words "ale shop." He met Corinne Robinson, Theodore Roosevelt's niece in Farmington, Connecticut, at the home of Roosevelt's older sister, Anna Roosevelt Cowles. They were married in a quiet ceremony in November of 1909 as the bride's younger brother, Stewart, had died in a fall from his Harvard dormitory room the previous February, and the family was still in mourning. It seems to have been a tradition in my family to name the second son after a dead uncle. My father was named for Stewart Robinson, and my brother Ian for Ian Hankey, my mother's only brother.

A sickly boy from birth, my father was the third of four children and the one most favored by Aggie, the Scottish nurse. Whenever he had to stay home from school because of his asthma and eczema, Aggie wrapped him in lotion-soaked cloths to soothe the itching and laid him out on the marble-topped table in the kitchen so he wouldn't miss out on the life of the house.

Theirs was a lifelong love affair. Aggie saved every scrap of paper, every school report, every messy art project, and every letter from boarding school that my father and his siblings ever produced. Many of Stewart's letters home from the war went directly to Aggie, and later when his trunk was shipped home to Avon from England, Aggie threw out all the letters my mother had written to him. Although Aggie protested that she thought the letters had come from other girlfriends, my mother thinks she did it on purpose, jealous that her favorite boy had finally married.

At the age of thirteen, like his father before him and his sons afterward, my father was enrolled at Groton, a private Episcopalian boarding school in a small town south of Boston. His early years there were not a success. When the headmaster, Rector Endicott Peabody, wrote to my grandparents about Stewart's untidy papers and his careless dress and manners, my grandfather made excuses for him, writing in response, *He has been ill almost all his life and the whole family have treated him as a semi-invalid.*

He pulled himself together the final year at Groton and graduated seventh in his class, but once released to the freedom of college, he slackened off again. At Yale, he joined the drama club, and when his younger brother John arrived at the college in 1933, the partying slipped into high gear. The two Alsop men were in demand as a sort of on-the-spot vaudeville team. Their most popular act was a Russian skit called "The Wooloffs" about a desperately poor woman who throws all her children from a horse-drawn sleigh to a pack of hungry wolves in order to keep the wolves from eating her, a performance which involved a great deal of drunken shouting in fake Russian accents.

His senior year at Yale, my father was suspended twice. Both incidents involved women and liquor, and the second was so egregious (taking a woman into a fraternity house at five o'clock in the morning) that he wasn't allowed to graduate with his class. When he moved to New York, he landed a job as an assistant editor at Doubleday, Doran Publishers—not surprisingly, since his cousin Ted Roosevelt (TR's son) was vice president of the company. His main interest seemed to be his social life, though in a letter home to Avon full of news about parties he'd been to or was planning to host, he also reported that he'd been allowed to retake his exams. In September, he was finally granted a Yale diploma. None of this checkered past was mentioned in 1973, when his Alma Mater awarded him an honorary doctorate for courage, insights, and "the common sense and civility you have steadily brought to bear on the chaos of our times."

In 1941, as war grew closer and more and more of his friends appeared in uniforms, my father began trying to enlist in every branch of the American Armed Forces. He and his brother John were both turned down for health reasons. Interestingly, my father's asthma history wasn't the primary reason he was rejected; rather, both he and John had hypertension, which was magnified by white coat syndrome. Every time someone strapped the cuff of the sphygmomanometer on one of their arms, their blood pressure shot through the ceiling. They decided the best way to fix this problem was to become thoroughly familiar with the instrument, so they bought one and took to testing each other day and night. It did no good.

In a definitive note from the adjutant general's office, my father was told that "Your tender of service is appreciated and has been made a matter of official record." It was the last thing he wanted to hear. His friends were starting to show up in New York bars in snappy military uniforms, and he'd become worried that as "a matter of official record," he'd end up pushing papers in some backwater office.

Early in 1942, he learned that a British regiment, the Kings Royal Rifle Corps, formed originally in colonial America as the Sixtieth Rifles, was taking a few American volunteers. His interview with Colonel Rex Benson at the British embassy in Washington turned out to be nothing but a formality, as the colonel was ready to sign him up on the spot.

When my father asked nervously about a medical exam, Benson waved his hand airily.

"Twenty-twenty vision?"

My father nodded.

"That's all we need to know. When you go over, my dear boy," the tall, mustachioed colonel advised, "be sure to take a dinner jacket and a shotgun for the grouse season." It turned out that Benson hadn't been in England since 1938, when life was considerably different.

THE ENGAGEMENT

MARCH–JULY, 1943

In the spring of her final year at Poles, my mother qualified to apply to Cambridge or Oxford, quite a feat for a sixteen-year-old girl. But it was deemed that war work was more important than women attending university, so only one week after that exciting kiss in the Mowbray's rose garden, she and Bee dutifully trundled off to a nine-month secretarial course at the Carr Saunders School in Broadway. Not long after the Carr Saunders offices in London had been destroyed in the Blitz, Francis David Charteris, the Earl of Wemyss and March (a name my mother never forgets) had offered Miss Carr and Miss Saunders his ancestral manor house in the Cotswolds. Stanway, an easy train ride to London and only ten miles from Granny Hankey's house, lay at the opposite end of England from my father's training camp in York. My mother felt that just as her real life should be starting, she'd been locked up in another school that was not much better than the convent.

But thanks to a scribbled address she'd given to my father the morning after the party at Allerton, he got back in touch. That fall, at their daughter's insistence, the Hankeys invited the American solder for dinner at 60 Pont Street one weekend when Tish was home from Stanway. It didn't go well. Granny, who'd always had her meals made by servants in Gibraltar, was not a good cook, especially when she had to make do with rations. Having just lost their only son, both of her parents were dead set against their teenage daughter having anything to do with this older man, the first American they'd ever met. But my father remained infatuated. At this dinner, their second meeting, he found my mother to be charming, gay, wonderfully naïve, and great fun. However, later that fall, when her parents refused to allow her to go alone with him to the British Museum or to attend his commissioning party at the Savoy Hotel, the eager suitor gave up the girl he liked to refer to as "Miss Moonlight and Roses." He wrote to his younger brother that his love life had come to a dead end though he continued to be sad about it since she was a real charmer.

"Well, you can't really blame your parents for not letting you go," I say to my mother when she tells me the story. "You were only sixteen and he was twenty-eight. I wouldn't have let you go."

She laughs. "Me neither," she says.

I used the great difference in their ages to my advantage when the man I was later to marry invited me out on my first date. We were visiting my aunt in Maine at the time and my mother, lying in a bubble bath, said absolutely not, she would not allow me to go to the dance with him.

"He's four years older than you are," she had said. "He's finishing freshman year in college." I was fourteen at the time, leaving in a month for my first year in boarding school.

"And how old were you when you met Daddy?"

She rolled her eyes. "That was different. Wartime."

"And how old was he?"

She gave in but insisted that my younger cousin go with us. Unbeknownst to her, Anne, brought up in Paris and far more sophisticated than I, spent most of the time necking with her boyfriend in the back seat of the car while I sat stiffly in the front and fiddled with the radio dial, hoping the music and my chatter would block out the sound of their moaning.

Early in March of 1943, Tish's mother, Cecilia, was standing in the ration line at Harrod's when her friend, Mrs. Tufnall announced that her daughter, Rosie, was pregnant and would be going down to the country for her confinement. Would Tish like Rosie's job in the Passport Control Office?

Tish definitely would. She leapt at the chance to get out of secretarial school and on with her life before the whole world blew up. Now that Hitler had turned his attention to the Eastern Front and London felt safer, Cecilia was eager to have her only daughter close by.

On March 17, 1943, her seventeenth birthday, my mother reported for the job at 55 Broadway in London. She was directed upstairs to the third floor, where under the stern eye of a Captain Hastings, she signed the Official Secrets Act. Although it was wartime, she did find it odd that young women handing out passports had to sign that document. Imagine her surprise when Captain Hastings ordered her to report immediately to Captain Russell on the fifth floor. That was when she finally learned the true nature of the work: she would be trained as a decoding agent for the naval division of MI5, the British counterintelligence and security agency.

Her job was to evaluate the reports that came in from British agents about movements up and down the coast. Each spy was rated as to their reliability, so my mother and the other young women in the office (their division was nicknamed the nursery) were trained to decide which reports were credible enough to send along to the admiralty.

However, the most exciting moment in her personal life came just two days later when she was presented at the Queen Charlotte Ball, the annual debutante dance at which seventeen-year-old girls from the British upper-classes were introduced to society with the express purpose of finding them eligible husbands. Lady Mowbray gave a dinner party in honor of Bee and Tish, but Bee caught chicken pox from my mother—who recovered in time for the party—while poor Bee had to stay in bed and miss the whole thing. My mother was wearing a ruffled dress by Molyneux, a famous Parisian designer who'd moved to London for the duration of the war. The wasp waist, the butterfly ruffles of the dress which highlighted her slender arms, and the deep red lipstick all contributed to the impression that, although she was one of the debutantes, she had to be older than seventeen.

After my father's big blowout commissioning party in December—the one my mother was not allowed to attend—he'd been billeted in grim Leeds, miles from anywhere. Although he was still serving with two of the other five Americans in the regiment, his favorites—Tom Braden and Ted Ellsworth—had been assigned to other platoons. For the time being, the wild parties they'd all enjoyed at the Cavendish Hotel while on leave in London had come to an end. In a letter to his younger brother John, he admitted to bedding some "hefty Irish colleens" who were the cousins of a screwball Irishman he met in a local bar, but for the most part he stuck close to the base. However, at some time during the ten months he'd spent in England, he met another promising young lady, a twenty-one-year-old daughter of a baronet, "a real peaches and cream type" with no stuffy parents. Feeling his age, my twenty-nine-year-old father seemed eager to find himself a suitable wife in England since he'd failed so miserably with the chattering Long Island debutantes back home. In March, he was able to wrangle his first leave to London in three months so that he could escort this new lady to the Queen Charlotte Ball.

My mother spied him first. There he was, the man who'd romanced her in the rose garden, sitting in the balcony above the dance floor with an older woman in a slinky black dress. Before she could change her mind, my mother skipped upstairs and tapped him on the shoulder. He looked surprised and rather pleased while his companion glowered at the impetuous girl in satin ruffles. Pleading manners, my father excused himself from his companion and led my mother downstairs for one awkward dance. He'd never been able to keep time or master steps, either on the dance floor or the drill parade ground, possibly because he was tone deaf. (Growing up, we children weren't allowed to play music in the house not only because it disturbed his writing but because music sounded to him like chalk scraped the wrong way on a blackboard.)

Despite his clumsy footwork, that one dance knocked the baronet's daughter out of the running. There's no knowing whether it was my mother's sly smile and bedroom eyes or her audacity at inviting him to dance, but after my father escorted "Miss Peaches and Cream" home that evening, he never saw her again. And now that my parents had rediscovered one another, and my mother was a working woman living in London, the romance heated up. Even though she was staying at 60 Pont Street in the top floor flat with her parents, they weren't able to keep close tabs on her. They knew not to ask the exact nature of her job, but suspected Tish wasn't actually working for Passport Control since she had to come and go at odd hours and often reported to the office on weekends. She soon became acquainted with all the top nightclubs, and because they operated out of the basements of buildings, her parents figured she was just as safe there during a raid as in the box room in the cellar at 60 Pont Street. And if she were being entertained for dinner, it meant one less meal her mother had to worry about on their limited rations. So they let her make her own plans without too many questions, and it seems they had no idea what was happening right under their noses.

In July, only four months after their chance meeting at the ball, my father received orders to ship out to North Africa where eleven months before, Ian Hankey had been dive-bombed by a Stuka in the western desert. For Stewart and his fellow soldiers of the Kings Royal Rifle Corps, Africa was nothing more than a way station on the way to the fight in Italy. Before Stewart boarded the SS *Volendam*, he wrote his mother a letter marked PRIVATE in large bold letters. He told her that he was engaged to be married on a post-war basis to "Miss Moonlight and Roses," who he referred to only once as Tish. His mother had spies everywhere, even in England, and he wanted to be sure the engagement remained a secret so that if he didn't survive the war, my mother would be completely free to choose another husband. Although he described the Hankeys, he didn't admit that Tish hadn't told them either. But he did go on about her.

She's shy in public and at first, extremely silent, but she's really great fun, not in the cocktail party sense of the word, but with a kind of private gayety.[sic] *Like all English girls, she seems distinctly uneducated in the academic sense, but she likes to read, and is essentially intelligent. To me she seems damn near perfect, and everyone else I know who's met her thinks almost as much of her as I do.*

My Connecticut grandmother's secretary retyped all my father's letters from the war, and a few years ago, my mother had them Xeroxed and bound, one copy for each one of us children. This letter wasn't included among those, and when I discovered it in the basement, it was lying on top of a love letter he must have written to my mother at almost the same time. I sat on the linoleum floor next to the washing machine, reading and re-reading words I couldn't imagine my father ever writing:

You really are a most amazing girl, darling. I have to keep telling you that so you won't forget it. Not just because you have this devastating charm I also have to keep telling you about. Others have that, not many, but some. But what is amazing is that I've never discovered in you a single affectation or insincerity. Which is amazing, take it from one who knows. Anyway I think you're absolutely wonderful, which you've probably guessed by now, so I won't embarrass you anymore by repeating it.

The man of these romantic letters is not a person I knew. By the time I came along, my parents had moved to America, the children were coming thick and fast, and he was under enormous pressure as a writing partner to a demanding older brother and a figure on the national political stage. He was a man who kept his personal and his public lives so strictly divided that when he came to write his own memoir, *Stay of Execution*, in his late fifties, the editor had to force him to talk about his six children.

He did compose another kind of love letter to my mother in his *Newsweek* column on August 30, 1971, two months after he was diagnosed with incurable leukemia and had been given six weeks to live. (I was twenty-six and pregnant with his first grandchild, the girl he didn't live long enough to meet.) In this piece, entitled "God Tempers the Wind," he describes the moment when he reaches for his wife's hand in the middle of the night. Falling in love and the specter of an early death broke through his normal reserve.

But my time with him, for the most part, fell between those two poles. The man I knew avoided all outward displays of affection. He often seemed surprised to look up from his paper in the evening and see that not only had he fathered six children, but a good number of them were wrestling on the floor at his feet.

These days, I am tempted to keep these letters to myself because I'm afraid my mother, upstairs in the garden room with her afternoon cup of heavily sugared coffee, will insist I stop digging into her private life. But in the end, the dutiful daughter prevails over the writer, greedy for every detail.

"You read them to me," she says, when I describe what I've found. She complains daily that something's gone wrong with her eyes, but the tests come back fine. I think she can't remember the beginning of a sentence by the time she gets to the end of it.

She leans forward to listen and when I'm done, she smiles. "Well, of course, I never saw the letters your father wrote to your grandmother."

"And what about this one he wrote to you?" I ask, showing her the letter I found in the basement. "Do you remember getting it?"

She shrugs, but the smile remains.

"He was such a romantic," I say.

"All so long ago," she muses in a dreamy voice.

After a brief silence, she reverts to her favorite topic of the moment—how she cannot stand that red poinsettia someone sent her two months ago, but luckily it sits behind her chair so she only has to see it when she walks in, not when she's sitting down.

"Why don't you throw it out?" I ask.

"Well, I'm doing my best to kill it." With looks and nasty thoughts, I guess, as she can no longer garden, even though she tells everyone how she pruned the dogwood outside the garden door and how she put in those new shrubs last fall. We understand this is her way of maintaining some belief that she controls her own life.

❧

Wartime romances and sudden engagements on the eve of battle are not uncommon, but my parents' marriage did seem precipitate. She was seventeen and he was twenty-nine. He'd been around the block. She'd been cloistered. She was a poorly educated, "penniless" Catholic and not, as he originally thought, the daughter of a belted earl. He was a well-connected American who planned to take her away from all she knew and loved.

I can understand at this distance what drew my father to my mother and caused him to pour out his love on paper. The physical beauty was always there, and still is. And he, for one, appreciated her reserve, her inscrutability. In describing her to his mother, he'd said: *She is utterly without affectation. I've never discovered her in one of those coy insincerities which usually accompany prettiness at seventeen, or at any age.*

My mother may be without guile, but she can also be completely without grace. If she doesn't like a present, she'll tell you to your face. If she thinks you're going to help her down the steps, she'll bark at you to get back or wave you away with a crutch. She hates formal acknowledgements of her age or large family celebrations, especially one that might put the spotlight on her. After we insisted on an "all-hands-on-deck" birthday weekend in Santa Fe to honor her on her seventy-fifth birthday, she showed her appreciation during the party, but muttered to me as we were leaving, "Thank God, we don't have to do that again."

A few years later, my son-in-law, who didn't know her very well at the time, organized the waiters in her favorite Italian restaurant to sing to her over dessert. The moment her chocolate mousse was served, with "Happy Birthday" scrawled in raspberry coulis around the edge of the plate, she noisily set about scratching out the greeting with her fork, so that halfway through the song, the waiters' voices melted into an embarrassed silence.

The gracelessness has gotten worse with age, and of course, some of it goes along with whatever form of dementia she has, but this is not unfamiliar behavior. My father, so used to the banalities of the courtships of his time, found her honesty refreshing; my brothers and I cringe at the sharp tone in her voice, the rude retort. A civility, a little white lie now and then, wouldn't kill her.

Far Apart

July 1943–March 1944

The first week of August 1943, Stewart shipped out on the SS *Volendam*, a troop carrier bound for Cairo. He sailed past Tish's childhood home, where on one side of the ship, Gibraltar was shrouded in darkness, while Algeciras, just up the coast in neutral Spain, blazed with lights—a strange sight for the British troops after fifteen months of observing England's nocturnal blackouts.

To keep her beloved safe, Tish had given him her brother's St. Christopher medal, which had been returned to his family from the western desert of North Africa along with his other effects. Somewhere off Gibraltar, the medal slipped from my father's neck and dropped into the sea. He became convinced that this bad omen meant he wouldn't return, but, as I pointed out to my mother years later, Uncle Ian died wearing the medal and Daddy survived, having lost it. She acknowledged my comment with a wry grin.

After taking a Vickers machine gun course in the desert and wandering around North Africa for a couple of months, my father and one of his four closest friends were assigned to the Eleventh Battalion. By mid-October, they were fighting with the Fifth Army in Taranto, Italy.

My mother tells me decades later that she wrote my father almost every day he was in North Africa and Italy, but many of those letters never reached him. The ones that did were inadvertently or deliberately tossed out by his old nurse, Aggie, when they arrived in Avon at the bottom of my father's army trunk after the war.

How I would have loved a look at my mother's letters to her secret fiancé. As hard as it is for me to imagine my restrained father as a romantic, it's truthfully more difficult to picture my mother—steeped as she was in the stiff upper lip ways of her British ancestors—pouring out her love in letters.

Unlike the Alsops, the Hankeys were not letter-writers. They wrote one another only when necessary, when news of an arrival or departure had to be reported or plans had to be made. Uncle Ian's letters from boarding school and later from the front are filled with spelling and grammatical errors, and although he refers to the letters his parents wrote to him, none of them survived. When it came to correspondence, my mother was a Hankey. During my seven years in boarding school and college, the letters I got from her contained practical information about travel plans and doctor's appointments. She always warned us not to leave anything at home when we departed for our next semester as she couldn't stand mailing boxes.

While my father was traveling to Africa, his younger brother John was steaming toward England, having finally gotten into the American army as a military policeman. Soon after John arrived in Wiltshire, he contacted Tish as Stewart had instructed. Whenever either one of them heard from my father, they wrote or cabled the other with his news. My uncle saved those letters from her, and fifty years later he mailed them back to her.

I have the feeling that my mother wrote nobody else letters that were as intimate and honest as the ones to John, whom she hoped would one day be her brother-in-law. Whatever his responses, they must have encouraged her to keep up the correspondence with the younger brother she had yet to meet. When I ask now about John and London, and that time when Daddy was away, she says dreamily, "We had a wonderful time then, John and I." Since they only met twice for dinner during the eight months my father was gone, I expect the regular correspondence is what makes her remember that time with such affection.

My father's comment that my mother *seems distinctly uneducated in the academic sense* rings true when I read her letters to

John. She uses almost no punctuation at all, and often is writing in such a rush that she drops crucial words or misdates her letters. I can sense the nervousness of this seventeen year old girl, who's well aware she's scribbling notes to a member of a very literate family. In an early apology to John, she asks him to *have the goodness to forgive this letter but not having the gift that the Alsop family has for writing I feel more than somewhat at a loss.*

Some of her phrases are familiar to me, the daughter reading them almost seventy years later. *Do be an angel,* she says at one point, when she's asking John to choose his favorite wines from a list. (To this day, she'll say to me, "Do be an angel and bring me my purse.")

She tells John about people who annoy her, and they are most often the people closest to her. This too is familiar. Not long after Stewart shipped out, Cecilia had a hysterectomy and went down to her mother-in-law's house in the Cotswolds to recover, leaving Tish and her father living together for three months. She writes John that her father hadn't told her that one of Stewart's letters had arrived until after she'd finished cooking dinner. *He said that he didn't like the idea of everything getting burnt, very sound my father but it annoyed me at the time.* And another time: *Life is very trying and so is Daddy I nearly murdered him this morning.* (I wonder from this distance whether she sensed that her father had his own secret life, although she didn't have concrete evidence of the long-term affair he was carrying on with his assistant until after the war.)

Only a few weeks ago, when my mother learned from her secretary Jan that none of us children would be able to visit on her birthday, she muttered, "Well, it's a good thing. If they came, I'd probably murder them." Jan was mystified by this comment, but I put it down to her hatred of celebrations. Even though I've heard her say she's doing her best to kill the poinsettia or she's going to murder this person or that for what seems like a harmless offense, I've never quite gotten used to the vehemence of my mother's vocabulary when annoyed.

❧

The two times when John managed to get some leave, he traveled down to London to take my mother out to dinner and the theater. He was struck with her efficiency at getting them into private nightclubs and wrote home to Avon that she was a real charmer (this seems to have been the Alsop boys' highest praise), mature for her age, a young woman with a lovely figure and face, and a somewhat elfin expression around the mouth.

After his second visit, my normally unemotional mother wrote that *even when you are 102 and I am 92, I shall continue to send you Christmas presents, you've no idea how wonderful it is to have you around not only as a link with Stew, but for yourself, it makes a terrific difference.* The special bond forged between them during those wartime years lasted until my uncle John's death sixty years later.

For the eight months that my father was away in Italy and North Africa, my mother struggled with the everyday troubles of a city at war. When a house down the street burst into flames, she and a friend who was staying over went out to watch the firemen and ended up dragging furniture out of the smoky building at one in the morning. They had no heating at home and little at the office, where twice that cold winter the boiler burst, forcing the staff to do their work with frozen fingers, dressed in coats and boots.

One weekend day, Tish and her parents decided to take a break from the gray, bombed-out views of London. They packed a picnic and caught a train out to Surrey to wander the grounds of Fetcham Park, where Arthur had spent his childhood and Tish had played as a three-year-old. The tenants greeted them warmly and showed the family around. The anatomy and physiology departments of University College, London, were leasing Fetcham since their buildings in London had been destroyed in a bombing raid. Air raid shelters had been dug in the front of the house, but other than that, the place appeared much the same as they remembered—that is, until Tish and her parents rubbed circles in the grimy garage windows. Inside, in neat lines, lay the embalmed bodies of dead soldiers. The corpses, contributed by families to the medical school, were awaiting autopsies by medical students as part of their training. Tish and her parents returned to their Pont Street flat in London quite shaken by their country outing. They never went back to Fetcham.

Meanwhile, when Bee graduated from the Stanway secretarial course, Tish managed to get her a job as a decoder in army intelligence on the floor above hers. As there was no room in the Pont Street flat, Bee moved into the Monkey Club, a nearby establishment which housed proper young women who came to London to do war work. The two friends traveled back and forth on the Underground to their offices whenever they were assigned the same shifts. Bee's brother, Charles Mowbray—who was training with the Grenadier Guards at Sandhurst—was only eighteen months older than Bee, so his friends were the right age for the two attractive decoding agents. Tish didn't let her secret engagement keep her from a whirling social life. Ever the efficient manager, she was known as the person who could get people into the best restaurants and nightclubs in wartime London.

Many days she admitted to boredom, fogged up in an office, smoking like a chimney and scribbling notes in a shorthand she couldn't even read. She wondered in a letter to John why she hadn't joined the WRENS, the women's division of the Royal Navy. But there were moments of excitement.

One Sunday in late September, my mother was alone at the office. The younger ones in the division had all come down with the flu and Miss Thring, Captain Russell's secretary, was taking a rare day off. My mother had been instructed to do her work in Captain Russell's office in case there were any calls. They must have been expecting something because the phone did ring. When my mother picked it up, the Scottish agent, reporting from the Outer Hebrides, suggested they "scramble," which meant they each pushed the extra button on their receiver to ensure that their conversation would be unintelligible to anybody tapping the line. He told her that their most reliable Norwegian agent had reported that the SS *Tirpitz* had been sunk. One of the largest battleships in the German fleet, the *Tirpitz* had disrupted Allied shipping for months from its position anchored against the side of a fjord in Norway. My mother scribbled the message in her terrible shorthand and as soon as they rang off, she called the director of naval intelligence's office in the admiralty and relayed the information to the deputy director. Then she rushed upstairs to find Bee, the only person she could safely tell. (In fact, the *Tirpitz* did not sink that day, but because the attack had done serious damage, the ship wasn't able to leave her anchorage again for seven months.)

Right there on the sixth floor of the MI5 building, the two friends danced a triumphant jig. They weren't exactly spies, but on a day like this, it was at least clear that they were helping defeat the enemy, a heady thought for a couple of teenagers. It made up in part for the dull days in the smoky office when nothing much seemed to happen.

Preparations

March–June 1944

After three months of real fighting in Italy, Stewart came back to England by way of North Africa. In the late summer of 1943, he'd left "Blighty's shores" as he liked to call it in his letters as a platoon leader in the Kings Royal Rifle Corps. He returned eight months later attached to an airborne unit called the Special Air Services. By the end of March, he was stationed at Milton Hall, eighty miles north of London, training with the Office of Strategic Services, (known as the OSS to parachute behind enemy lines into France.

Soon after his arrival, he managed to get a week's leave and made a beeline for London. Within days, he wrote home to his parents that he and Tish were trying to convince her parents that they should marry right away. He'd finally divulged his fiancée's full name and had already solicited reference letters to her stuffy English father from John Winant, the American ambassador, and his cousin and former employer, Ted Roosevelt, the president's son, a brigadier general serving with the American First Infantry.

Roosevelt responded immediately with a hand-scrawled note to Mr. Hankey, mentioning all of his associations with Stewart and lauding him *as honorable, hardworking and very intelligent. Among other things he's a delightful companion.* But he made the fatal mistake of assuming that the two were already engaged. Mr. Hankey was not pleased.

My daughter is not officially engaged to Stewart and before anything is arranged, we must go into all questions of finance, marriage settlements etc. as, if my daughter does marry him, it will of course mean her living in America and away from us, and one would naturally want to know that she is to an extent independant (sic). *I understand he gave up a good job to come over and join the British army and I sincerely hope that after the war he will be able to go back to it or to something better.*

Ted minced no words when he forwarded this letter to his cousin Stewart.

Dear Stew,

I enclose a letter that came from your pa-in-law to be. If I were you, I'd tie a rock about the old bastard's neck and throw him in a pond. There's a certain type of middle-class Englishman who doesn't understand courtesy. He thinks it implies a feeling of inferiority on your part and acts accordingly. The only way to do with them is to insult them at once and then they assume you are their superior and also act accordingly.

It's a happy thought that you and Patricia will be in the U.S. and he in England.

It was clear that the Hankeys did not consider this American soldier to be anybody special, no matter who he could round up to support his cause. In the meantime, Tish knew that, at the very least, her father expected Stewart to make a formal request for her hand, so she figured out a way to bring the two men together.

Since Mrs. Hankey was still recuperating from surgery down in the country, Tish, Stewart, and Grandfather Hankey went out for lunch at the Berkeley Hotel, where they all fiddled with the bread and tried to make small talk. They then took the London Tube to the Kew Gardens stop, where by pre-arrangement, Tish trotted off to feed the ducks while Stewart made his case to my grandfather.

From a distance, she could see how nervous and unhappy these two shy men looked. Neither one seemed to know what to do with his hands or feet. They shuffled and muttered to each other, and when she returned, they didn't say a word to her about what had transpired between them. From the looks on their faces, she assumed that some agreement had been reached.

Letters began to fly back and forth between England and Avon, Connecticut, about the terms of a dowry. It was decided that Stewart had to *beard the lion in her den* as he wrote home. He and Tish took the train down to Broadway in the Cotswolds, hoping to convince Mrs. Hankey that her daughter, who'd just turned eighteen, should be allowed to marry this American soldier twelve years her senior, who was about to parachute into occupied France. They'd taken the precaution of inviting John to join them, but he was to come along a few days later.

My father, thanks to Aggie's spoiling and the attentions of the batman (valet) that the British army provided for its officers, had not learned to take care of himself. Neither his attention to his personal dress nor his manners had been improved by two years in the army. Also, he'd managed to leave most of his belongings in Naples almost two months before, and so was dressed in bits and pieces of the British uniform borrowed from his fellow soldiers. From the moment my father met my mother, he sensed that she could manage him quite well, and vowed that he would never be tempted to throw a boot at her—the way he usually dealt with people who tried to manage him. That said, there was little she could do to convince her own mother that this prospective husband was the right one for her. My grandmother had met him once or twice before, but because of the British uniform, she'd never really believed that he was an American. Granny held the combined prejudices of a narrow Catholic and a narrow Englishwoman who believed that God made the English upper classes specifically to rule mankind and that all other nations were "lesser breeds before the law."

My father began to bridle under the insinuation that because he wasn't English, he couldn't be a gentleman. Everybody in the predominantly female household appeared to be against the marriage, and my father was ready to start a real fight when, just in time, Uncle John arrived. The opposite of his older brother, John was all spit and polish. His shoes shone like mirrors, his trousers were creased to a knife-edge, and his manners were impeccable. He charmed the ladies with stories about the farm in Avon and the Roosevelt relations so well that the following day, Mrs. Hankey pulled Tish aside and suggested that she was marrying the wrong brother.

"What did you say?" I ask my mother when she tells me this story.

"I told her that wouldn't work because first of all, he hadn't asked me to marry him, and secondly, I wasn't in love with him."

Despite Cecilia's clear disappointment in her choice, my mother and the two Alsop brothers left for London with the feeling that the Hankeys would agree to the marriage once the details of the dowry had been worked out, and that the wedding would take place after the war. My mother and father, however, had other ideas.

The day Tish accompanied her betrothed and George Thomson, his good friend, to Euston Station for the train to their camp in Peterborough, she wrote directly to her future mother-in-law in Connecticut for the first time. She reported to Mrs. Alsop that Stew was looking very brown and fit, and despite the crowds at the station, he and George had found seats on the train. She signed her letter, Yours sincerely, Patricia Hankey. From then on, she kept up a regular correspondence with Stewart's mother—an act of considerable bravery.

Because the Alsop family shared each letter from one with all the other branches, Tish had seen the missives flying back and forth from Stew's older brother Joe—a journalist serving in China with the Flying Tigers, an American volunteer group recruited by Claire Chennault, a retired U.S. army captain, to fight the Japanese in Burma and China during 1941–42—to her own future father-in-law, a dairy farmer and beekeeper, who especially enjoyed mocking the Roosevelt administration when writing to his three politically left-wing sons. The Alsops described events, argued political points, revealed their emotional states, and made arrangements, all with equal gusto. Unlike the Hankeys, they wrote easily and fluently, a habit developed through generations. When my mother wrote to Mrs. Alsop in Avon, she was acutely aware, once again, of her youth, her lack of education, and her desire to impress the woman who would one day be her mother-in-law.

My father was attached to a secret commando arm of the OSS. called the Jedburghs. Teams of three were being trained to parachute into occupied France and harass the Germans soon after the Allied landing in France. In the late spring of 1944, everybody was gearing up for that day.

The OSS, founded by the World War I hero "Wild Bill" Donovan, was responsible for running clandestine activities from training resistance fighters in Indochina to dropping operatives behind enemy lines in Germany. The Jedburgh operation was the first in which Americans worked directly with their British counterpart, Special Operations Executive (SOE), as well as with the French resistance movement, known as the Maquis. The name Jedburgh came from a place in Scotland where justice for sheep rustlers was said to mean, "Hang them first and question them afterward." It was a crafty way of alerting the trainees what they were in for if they were caught behind enemy lines.

In May, just one week after he turned thirty, my father was named the leader of Team Alexander, which consisted of himself, a twenty-year-old American radio operator named Dick Franklin, and René Thouville, a graduate of the prestigious French military academy Saint Cyr. The two Americans knew that Thouville was a nom de guerre but didn't press the man on particulars.

The three became close, eager to understand one another in whatever ways would help them survive in enemy territory. They devised inspired plans to outwit the training staff, which meant they spent hours hunkered down in hedgerows, telling jokes and getting to know one another. Thouville, a serious military man, was at first horrified by his commanding officer's irreverence. What kind of a British platoon leader was this, a man who exhorted him to relaxez vous and found ingenious ways to duck out of forced marches? But it didn't take him long to follow suit, and soon Thouville began to trade jokes with the other two, most of them revolving around strange fellows in insane asylums.

The other Americans in the Kings Royal Rifle Corps had

become my father's best friends when they trained together in York in 1942, but they'd all been split up after shipping out to North Africa. Now he was preparing to go back into battle, not under the cover of a platoon, but with two men he barely knew.

More and more, my mother's memory has continued to slip. Her short-term memory is almost completely gone. Now, when I have a cup of tea with her and go to the kitchen to get more hot water, she greets me on my return to the garden room as if I've just arrived after weeks away. Telephone calls are especially difficult because she can no longer hit the conversational ball back across the net.

But today we have one of our more lucid phone calls. As long as I stick to the past and to very specific details, and fill in some of the blanks, we can almost have a conversation.

"Do you remember—" I stop myself. I swore I would never use that verb with her again.

"Daddy called you at 60 Pont Street to say he could get married the next week."

"Well, he couldn't jump right away because that other man, the French man—"

"Thouville—"

"That's right, he broke his ankle. That delayed their…" she hesitates again.

"Their mission. They were training at Milton Hall in Peterborough?"

"Yes, once I went up to stay with a couple near his training camp."

"After you were married?"

"Yes," she says dreamily. "I remember the people were perfectly nice, but very suburban. They had antimacassars on the arms of the sofa." *Not our class, dear,* she is thinking, but I am thrilled that she's able to retrieve the word antimacassar. In fact, I don't think I've ever heard her use it.

A few days later, I read her some of the letters she wrote in

1944 to John and her future mother-in-law. To hear the sound of her own teenage voice coming across the phone thrills her. She laughs at her attempts at humor, her comments on her stuffy parents, and her insights into the man she'd agreed to marry. I can call her the next day and read her exactly the same letters, and she will get the same pleasure from them because she remembers nothing of our talk the day before. Sometimes I feel as if I'm introducing her to a teenage girl she'd forgotten ever existed.

I like living in the past with my parents, when they were young and brave, in the peak of health, unburdened by children, and ready to take on the world. It's so much easier than having tea with my mother in her eighties, still elegant but daily more unmoored even in her familiar surroundings.

In the end, my parents prevailed. Letters back and forth to Connecticut on the subject of a settlement reached no real conclusion, although my father did press his own father to come across with assurances that if he were to be killed jumping into occupied France, my mother would be provided for. Granny Hankey discovered she had known Bay Wolryche-Whitmore Scott, a cousin of my Connecticut grandmother since before the war. Even though Bay's father was a Protestant rector in a Gloucestershire church, she approved of the calling, if not the religion. And when Bay invited Granny Hankey around for tea, she went on about the distinguished ancestors of the Alsop family, which seemed to do much more to convince the Hankeys of my father's potential worth as a son-in-law than letters from ambassadors and brigadier generals named Roosevelt. In late May, an announcement of the engagement appeared in the London Times.

The long-awaited D-Day finally came, and it seemed that my father would be shipped out at any minute.

On Thursday June 14, the phone rang at 60 Pont Street. It was my father calling Tish to report that Thouville had hurt his ankle riding a motorcycle, so their departure had been delayed. If he could get his commanding officer to give him as much as a week's leave, they could get married the next Tuesday.

My mother, conscious of her parents listening in on her end of the conversation, told him to call back at the same time the next day, when she'd have the answer. Her father refused to tell her what he thought of the idea, but his response was not encouraging. "Your mother and I will discuss it, and let you know tomorrow."

Tish went to work as usual the next day, but she was so fidgety and out of sorts that her boss, Miss Thring, stopped by her desk to ask what the matter was.

"My parents are deciding today if I can marry my fiancé next week."

"Maybe you'd be better off at home."

"Oh no, I'd go mad waiting for them to make up their minds."

In a letter that she never saw until I found it decades later, my grandfather Hankey wrote my father and denied him permission to marry Patricia *in these terribly uncertain and quickly moving times*. Not long after Arthur Hankey had arrived in London in September of 1940, he was hired by the Ministry of Economic Warfare, the department that monitored the flow of supplies from both occupied and neutral countries. It's not clear when he started the affair with Clare, his secretary at the Ministry, but looking back, my mother is pretty sure he was living a double life for most of the war. As the fiction writer, I like to imagine that Clare, who must have typed this letter denying them permission, convinced Arthur to change his mind. Constrained as she was by the secret of her own affair, perhaps Clare wished to see another woman, even her lover's daughter, getting what she wanted.

That evening, when Tish and her parents reconvened, her father, always a deliberate man, started in on a long lecture. My mother, who felt as if she was going to jump out of her skin, interrupted him after the first sentence.

"Daddy," she cried, "Stew is going to call, and I never know when he can get to a phone, so please tell me your answer first, and then I'll listen to your lecture."

The answer was yes, followed by a disquisition on wartime marriages and rushing into this kind of lifetime commitment: she didn't know where she was going, she'd never been to America, she was very young, and people only get married once in life.

"Everything he said made perfect sense," my mother tells me years later. "Very reasonable points, every one of them."

Then they sat in tense silence until the phone finally rang.

"Colonel Musgrave says I can have six days leave starting Monday. What do your parents say?"

"They've agreed."

A silence.

"Jesus Christ," my father muttered under his breath. "Trapped like a rat." The carefree man about town, who'd sailed through life on charm and luck, had just come about and run into king-hood a shore he'd managed to avoid for years.

Those words became family legend, and every time through the years that my mother has retold the story, she's always added, "I could have murdered him."

Who could blame her?

THE WEDDING

The first V-1 to hit London landed on June 13, one week after the Normandy landings. The Allies had finally seized the offensive, so the onset of these pilotless rockets was especially demoralizing to the Londoners, weary from four years of intermittent bombing attacks. By the weekend of June 16, as many as sixty V-1s were reaching the capital daily.

Churchill ordered the air raid sirens to be turned off after the first week, as there wasn't enough time for people to get to a shelter. With bombing runs, you had warning from all the coastal defenses that the planes were coming, but that wasn't possible with V-1s. They came too fast. The steering apparatus was set so that the doodlebug, as the English dubbed it, either dropped like a stone when its fuel ran out or kept on gliding until it crashed. You could hear them coming, a strange whining sound which, after an oddly mechanical cough, suddenly cut out.

"If it stopped right over your head," my mother explained, "you prayed it had been set to glide. If it stopped somewhere behind, you prayed it would plummet straight down. Whatever happened, there was no time to run, just time for prayer. They were more nerve-wracking than the bombs."

Because of her decoding work, my mother had known for some time that something big was coming. The naval division had been gathering information about the rocket construction at Peenemünde, a German port on the Baltic Sea. Then reports from the agents listed a curious combination of transport materials: heavy water from Norway, ball bearings from Czechoslovakia, and so on. Weeks before the first rocket hit London, my mother had decoded a report about large, covered objects on flat cars shipped down to Pas de Calais, which remained the launching area for the V-1s until the Allies overran the site.

None of this stopped the wedding preparations. Accustomed as they were to "carrying on," the Hankeys swung into full gear on Saturday morning. Stewart was due to arrive Monday, and the wedding was scheduled for Tuesday.

Tish and her father took her birth certificate to the Chelsea town hall so she could apply for the marriage license. Because Tish, at eighteen, was still considered a minor, her father had to sign that he agreed to this wedding, which must have galled him after all his objections. The clerk then demanded to know the fiancé's mailing address and would not accept a post office box number. My mother stalwartly refused, citing the Official Secrets Act, until it became clear she wasn't going to get the license without divulging Stewart's location. She gave up the Milton Hall address without further protest.

"Great spy I'd make," came her wry remark years later.

Meanwhile Granny Hankey consulted with Father Anderson, the parish priest at St. Mary's Cadogan Street. As he hailed from the Hebrides, nobody could understand much of what he said, but he cleared his schedule so he could marry the couple on Tuesday in a small side chapel. Although Stewart had agreed that any children of the marriage would be brought up as Catholics, he himself refused to convert, and as Father Anderson liked to remind his parishioners, only Catholics are allowed to be married at the high altar. Since the high altar at St. Mary's had recently been bombed, it hardly seemed a matter worth emphasizing, but Granny Hankey didn't appreciate being reminded that her daughter was marrying not only an American, but a non-practicing Episcopalian American to boot.

As to the question of a wedding ring, the single solitaire diamond engagement ring from the Alsops still had not arrived, but Granny Hankey insisted that her daughter must have a 22-carat gold wedding band, not an easy thing to find in wartime London. However, after four years of functioning in a city where basic food and services were in short supply, Granny had developed shrewd methods for getting what she

needed. Somewhere she'd made a friend who worked in one
of the remaining jewelry stores in the Burlington Arcade, and
without too much ado, he produced a lovely, simple band that
fit perfectly, the one my mother wears to this day.

However, there was no time to find white material for a
wedding dress in any of the shops, so my mother dug up her
old tennis dress from her years at Poles. She'd reached her full
height of five feet, nine inches while still at boarding school
so the dress didn't have to be lengthened, only taken in—with
rations and general wartime anxiety, she'd lost weight. After the
landings in France, London had cleared out and hotel rooms
were once more available so a thousand-pound wedding wire
from Stewart's brother-in-law secured them the honeymoon
suite at the Ritz.

All my father had to do was show up with a best man. His
brother John was denied leave from parachute training school,
so Daddy chose his old friend and fellow soldier, George
Thomson. It seemed appropriate, after all, because George had
been there at the original meeting of the betrothed pair, twenty-one months earlier in Allerton Park, the Mowbrays' baronial
castle in Yorkshire.

Although Tish was granted a rare weekend day off on Saturday so she could prepare for the wedding, she and Bee had
both been ordered to report for work that Sunday. All four of
the young women who worked in the naval division were at
their posts in the decoding department on the fifth floor that
morning when, just before eleven o'clock, they heard the now
familiar whine of a V-1 overhead. Normally, the rockets came
in groups of five, but this was a loner, a rocket that had been
winged. It flew in a circle over the building and cut out right
above them. Everybody dove under their desks.

The explosion was tremendous and very close. When the
dust had cleared, Tish rushed up to the sixth floor, grabbed
Bee, and together they climbed the stairs to the roof of their
building at 55 Broadway. The flying bomb had hit the neigh-
boring Guards Chapel adjoining Wellington Barracks. The particular anguish of this explosion was that it came in the middle

of the memorial services for soldiers from five brigades who'd been killed in the war, so many of their family members were attending the sung eucharist in honor of their loved ones. From the adjoining roof, Tish and Bee witnessed a scene of complete devastation. The direct hit destroyed the roof and the supporting walls, and tons of rubble fell onto the congregation. The first rescue teams were unable to hack through the collapsed roof and smashed walls in order to administer morphine to the injured and dying, until finally someone found a way in through the back of the altar. Incredibly, the silver cross was untouched, the candles on the main altar continued to burn, and one of the few unhurt survivors was the Bishop of Maidstone, who was leading the service. The portico over the altar had protected him from the full force of the blast.

In all the conversations with my mother about her losses during the war, this moment hit her the hardest. On the eve of her own wedding, she stared down into what became an instant grave for so many.

On Monday, June 19, Stewart checked into the Cavendish Hotel for his last night as a single man. The Cavendish, on Jermyn Street in London, was still owned and operated by the legendary Rosa Lewis, but she was in her final days. Known as the "Queen of Cooks," and rumored to have been Edward the VII's lover, she had a soft spot for American soldiers, so Stew and his friends had spent many drunken leaves in the hotel, where Rosa often threw out other guests to make room for them. But even though they'd met my mother and liked her, every eccentric member of the staff—from Edith Jeffries, Rosa's efficient companion, to Moon, the night man, and Bennett, the butler— all took a very dim view of the institution of marriage. The day of the wedding dawned bright and beautiful, a lucky thing as it had done nothing but rain in England for the previous three weeks. That morning, Bennett led the unsuspecting groom-to-be into the "Dispense," their name for the liquor closet, with the suggestion that he might need a little fortification on this auspicious day. Then, without a word, he skipped nimbly out, locked the door behind him and called out words of comfort to my enraged father.

"You don't want to be getting married, Mr. Stewart. Not a good idea. I've tried it more than once and it's always ended badly. I'm saving you from a most unhappy fate, I promise you, sir."

Someone, probably the reliable Edith, finally heard the terrible racket issuing from the pantry and released the furious bridegroom, who tried to pull himself back together for the ceremony. George Thomson showed up just in time to straighten Stewart's tie, flatten his collar, and buff up his shoes. In the Kings Royal Rifle Corps dress uniform, complete with parachute wings at the right shoulder and the Sam Browne belt looped across his chest, my father looked every bit the noble British soldier.

A spray of pink and white peonies adorned the carved marble altar of the Blessed Sacrament Chapel in the corner of St. Mary's. Arthur Hankey hired a car to drive the family of three the few blocks from Pont Street to Cadogan Street where a photographer waited. The first official picture shows Tish in her platform heels standing next to her diminutive father. Grandfather Hankey looks quintessentially British with his clipped mustache, striped tie and double-breasted suit. A white carnation is tucked into the lapel just above the handkerchief peeking out of his left breast pocket. As Bee couldn't get off work that day, there is no one to catch the bouquet, so my mother has slipped the bunch of white stephanotis through the belt of her short-sleeved tennis dress. Her only jewelry, a string of pearls, lies flat against her notched collar. A white beret with a side bow modeled on the official hat of the Women's Royal Naval Service (officially known as the WRENS), tilts jauntily atop her curly hair so that the short tulle veil drifts down across her face to just above her shoulders. She wears dark lipstick which outlines her dazzling smile. She looks calm, slim, elegant and years older than eighteen.

Arthur Barnard Hankey and Tish on her wedding day. Credit: Portman Press Bureau

Despite another V-1 attack the morning of the wedding, the small party of guests arrived on time at the church. The American side was represented by a smattering of friends and fellow soldiers and two sinister-looking English cousins who glared at one another and everybody else from under their black hats. My father, who confessed in a letter home to being very nervous about the ceremony itself, managed to get the ring on the correct finger, and the priest offered the final blessing.

Outside the church once again, the photographer captures the couple with my mother's right arm through my father's left, her veil pushed back over the top of the cocky beret. Both are smiling, although his expression is shyer and more tentative than hers. His left fist is tightly clenched, as if now that he's finally got her, he's going to make sure he never lets her go. The photo shows a blackened fingernail on her middle finger, which must have been slammed in some door not too long before. The stephanotis spray remains tucked firmly in the same place on her belt as in the pre-marriage pictures. In her left hand, my mother is holding the official marriage license, which the priest has wisely entrusted to her instead of her new husband.

Tish and Stew on their wedding day.
Credit: Portman Press Bureau

For my mother, there was no receiving line as the party was simply too small. What must she have felt, milling around with the handful of guests, and introducing the Brits to the Americans? I can only imagine what was going through her mind.

I'm marrying the first man who ever kissed me. I hope to God he comes back from France because even though I don't know him very well, I do love him, and he is wild about me, and I don't want to be a young widow living with my parents forever. I want to go to America and start my life all over again as far away from dusty, dirty, bombed-out London as I can get.

The wedding party went on for a week. As soon as possible, they left the small reception by chauffeured taxi and checked into the luxurious bridal suite on the top floor of the Ritz, with a sweeping view of Green Park. Later that evening, they repaired to the bar in the basement, and when Stewart went off to telephone his younger brother John, Tish fell into animated conversation with a British officer. By mistake, the newlyweds had settled themselves in the corner of this establishment frequented by higher class prostitutes, so the moment Stewart returned from the phone box, he realized that the soldier chatting with his bride assumed he was making an assignation for the night. My mother was not as sophisticated as she pretended to be.

The next day, they met a friend at Claridge's for drinks and then repaired to the Hankeys' flat, so that my mother could cook dinner with her new husband's extra rations. Her exhausted parents had gone to the country for a brief respite from the wedding fuss and the V-1 attacks, which were coming over in regular waves, two or three an hour.

Another night, Tish, Stewart, and seven fellow soldiers walked down Picadilly to Les Ambassadeurs, one of their favorite hangouts. At the end of the week, John and his friend Reeve checked into the Cavendish, having completed their parachute course in Scotland. With very little delay, they scooped up Rosa, Edith, and one of Rosa's terriers named Kippy, along with a couple of fellow parachutists, and headed around the corner to join the honeymooners at the Ritz. The next day, Rosa sent flowers to the bride and groom with a note penned in her shaky handwriting with even shakier punctuation.

My dearest Friends, Cavendish is your home in all times of pleasure or not—take care of your dear selves I love you both always + loved my lovely dinner and time with you both and we will have it—write me as real old Rosa only the Cook Edith + I all way. Rosa Lewis

The partying never stopped and at some point, during the five-day honeymoon my mother asked her new husband whether they might have just one evening alone. He looked appalled at the suggestion and reminded her that this was his leave time, the only time he got to see others outside of the army. Considering what was coming at them in the next weeks and months, leave was sacred. Nobody was excluded from any party and no party should ever end.

"He was right," she told me years later with a shrug.

The top of the Ritz turned out to be the perfect place to watch the buzz bombs coming in, and one evening, as they were having drinks on the roof, a doodlebug whined its way over their heads. Everybody ducked and the rocket landed with a terrific explosion in the middle of Green Park, adjacent to the hotel. By the time they'd collected themselves, my father was discovered cowering in a stairwell, while his new bride, dressed in sexy black, hadn't moved from her place by the parapet. Although she admitted that she minded these rockets more than the bombs, Stewart and John found her to be remarkably unfazed by it all. Tish was not only a woman who would be able to manage my father, but at that moment she must have seemed to him capable of managing the war.

My mother was always at her best in a crisis.

The phone ringing in my New York apartment pulls me away from my parents on that London rooftop in June. It's the physician's assistant who makes house calls, reporting that my mother has a stage-2 pressure wound, which I learn is the clinical term for a bedsore.

"Her lungs are clear although the heart murmur, of course, continues to be quite pronounced, which is not a surprise," says the young woman. "I'll order a new gel mattress, which Medicare will pay for. I can also see if they will cover gel pillows for the wheelchair and the chair she uses in the garden room."

It's disorienting to be talking about heart conditions and bedsores when I'm imagining my young mother dancing the nights away in the arms of her new husband, surrounded by parachutists, all of them ready to go operational at any moment. In her own way, right now, she's ready to go operational too. Between us, we have made all the preparations any person can make on this side of the divide. I can manage her care from a distance, and we've alerted doctors, nurses, and caregivers that she wants to die at home. We'll see.

But I want to stay in London in 1944.

THE MARRIAGE BEGINS

JUNE–OCTOBER 1944

My father didn't leave for France until early August, so the newlyweds had another month of weekends in London. One time, my mother took the train up to Peterborough, near his camp. Traveling by train in wartime Britain meant you could never predict your arrival time because whenever the air raid siren went off, British Rail stopped the trains until the all-clear sounded. In the days of the V-1s, the schedule grew even more erratic. Black shades covered the windows, and the only light came from tiny flickering bulbs. But my teenage mother loved it. Everybody smoked, and so did she, because if you were going to stink of smoke anyway, you might as well enjoy the cigs yourself. The British soldiers, known affectionately as Tommies, squatted on their rucksacks in the corridors because there were never enough seats. My thin mother, with her big brown eyes and shy smile, chatted with the soldiers, changed around so they could have a comfortable seat, accepted their lights, flirted, and didn't bother to mention her husband.

In Peterborough, she and my father spent two nights with an elderly couple who'd offered to take in married guests for weekends. That Sunday, the feast day of St. Thomas More, she dragged my father to church with her. The boring priest droned on about the life of St. Thomas, and when he said, "Now let us consider the other saints we can celebrate this day," my father began to twitch and roll his eyes, so right after Communion, they slipped out the side door.

In one of his last letters home before he left for France, my father asked his mother to buy his wife some underclothes. As he put it, "ladies' more intimate garments" couldn't be found anywhere in England and by that time, my mother's, although clean, were falling apart. He sent her measurements— "Chest thirty-two and a half inches, waist twenty-five and a half inches, hips thirty-three and a half inches"—after noting proudly that he'd taken them himself. Neither one of them knew yet that she was already pregnant.

Anybody in England who signed the Official Secrets Act during the war took it very seriously. All through their courtship, my mother had maintained the fiction that she worked for Passport Control, but on the last night they spent together, she finally told my father that she was employed as a decoding agent for the secret intelligence service. She only divulged this information to him then so he would know, if he never returned, that she too had been contributing to the war effort in a significant way. It also meant she could tell him that she'd be able to track his movements in France, as they could send messages to each other through Major Henry Coxe, Jr., the American Special Forces Headquarters (SFHQ) officer who shared overall command of the Jedburgh teams with a British lieutenant colonel. Coxe was well aware of the young Mrs. Alsop's position at MI5. His office was located in Baker Street, and through official channels, he promised to let her know whenever he had news of Stewart or John, who'd dropped into France the third week of July.

Oh, and there was one more thing.

"My period is late. But don't get excited," she said to her new husband. "I'm very erratic."

And then he was gone. She was back at the office, smoking with the other young ones, ducking under her desk when they heard a buzz bomb overhead, dutifully returning home to 60 Pont Street at night because, after all, now she was a married woman. No more bouncing around to the nightclubs or flirting with the few soldiers still left in town, now that every man in uniform had gone across the Channel.

In late August, she wrote to the mother-in-law she'd never met to announce that she was expecting a baby, due in March, and that because of the erratic communications with the Jedburgh teams in France, Stew didn't know for sure that she was pregnant, although she'd told him that it was a possibility before he left. She was sure he'd be as thrilled as she was. At the end of the letter, she reported she'd heard through official channels that Stew was fine and heading for Paris, which she noted, *must be a strange mixture of merrymaking and street fighting all going on at the same time.*

At one point during my father's almost three-year battle with leukemia, we children were all called home to have our blood tested. The doctor wanted to see if we could donate platelets to Daddy, as that clotting factor in his blood was so consistently low that he was in danger of bleeding to death should he cut himself. And since he was still playing tennis and was famous for whacking his lower shin bone with his racket at the end of his vicious cutting serve, this was a real concern. The doctor, who'd become a good friend of mine, took me aside to tell me that although I couldn't donate platelets to my father, should I ever need to give blood to my mother, I was a perfect match for her. This didn't surprise me.

In my freshman year at college, I'd taken the train into New York to meet with a doctor who asked few questions and dispensed birth control pills to anybody willing to pay his fee. A few months later, at home for vacation, I climbed up on a stepladder to get some dishes from a high shelf for the Latina maid who was too short to reach them herself. When my mother came into the kitchen, she blurted out, "Good God, are you pregnant?"

Apparently, my varicose veins resembled hers, blue bulging ropes snaking down the backs of my legs. I hadn't noticed. By that time, my mother had already survived two blood clots: one in her lung, and the other in her leg.

She made an appointment with her vein doctor, who asked me the same question. I confessed to him what I didn't dare tell her—that I was on birth control pills.

He shook his head. "Get off them immediately. With your mother's history, you're in danger of blood clots."

So that was the end of easy birth control for me. As it turned out, I inherited my mother's fertility along with her blood.

Although she got news every few weeks from Major Coxe that my father was still alive, the first time she heard from him directly was through a letter he managed to send out of France with a returning paratrooper in late September. He gave her a few details of his adventures, including the fact that he'd jumped out of the plane much too early, at eight-hundred feet, and wandered alone through occupied France for a night and a day before being reunited with his team. He promised to tell her all when he returned, and joked that in the years to come, she'd be thoroughly sick of the stories that started with the line, "when I was with the French Maquis." She was relieved to read how eager he was to get home to her. *I had to be here for a month, and to see some very ugly things, to realize how lovely and good you are and how deeply I love you.*

What he didn't know was that late one night in early September of 1944, she'd begun to bleed and was in such pain that her father convinced the doctor to come through a V-1 raid and the pouring rain to the top of 60 Pont Street to confirm the miscarriage. He wrote out a prescription that her father managed to fill at the all-night pharmacy in Piccadilly Circus. Later, the doctor said that she'd lost the baby because after two years of rations, she was too thin and anemic. She and her mother traveled down to an aunt's house in the Cotswolds in the hopes that the young bride might rest and put on a little weight before her husband came home, whenever that might be.

Stewart's letter referred to the possible baby as Joe the VI and guessed that, since he'd had no message from Henry Coxe, she wasn't pregnant after all which left her alone to mourn for the lost baby. The pattern of solitary mourning would be repeated in the years to come.

I'm getting messages from various people that my mother is in pain. She brushes it off in our phone calls, but then she's always kept that stiff upper lip attitude, especially with me. It comes, I believe, from her genuine desire not to be a burden. I often teased her that her epitaph should read, NO POINT FUSSING. No longer. We're too close to the graveyard to laugh about it anymore.

But my cousin, another friend, and her caregiver all report that she has black circles under her eyes, that she is more irritable, that she says she can't get comfortable at night, and that it's hard for her to sleep. Zuni began to count how many Percocet pills she was taking. Mummy, who says she really doesn't need the painkillers, had taken twenty-one pills in nine days, close to three per day. My mother has always trusted doctors and pills to take care of her aches and pains. How do I make her feel that her pain is taken care of, and at the same time convince her to go off the Percocet? I order all the medications be moved to the kitchen and dispensed only at regular times.

This latest chipping away at her independence infuriates her, although she doesn't confront me directly about it. She tells a friend that her daughter is trying to get her off painkillers. This is true, and the thought keeps me awake at night. If she needs to blame someone, I can accept that it will be me, especially since I'm not there every day. But I hate the idea that she's hurting, and I worry that the front-line caregivers will suffer because of decisions I'm making from two hundred fifty miles away.

At the same time, it takes me back to the little girl who was scared of her crazy mother, even though I didn't know it was alcohol that created so much of the tension and despair in our house. With decisions like this one, I've become the big sister again, the one who had to protect my younger brothers from the bizarre, maudlin clinging, the weepy declarations of love that the liquor released from that deeply sad, abandoned place inside my mother. I have to remind myself that I don't need to protect Zuni and Jan. They're not my little brothers. They didn't experience my mother as children the way I did. They can take care of themselves.

The pain in Mummy's back and hips started seventy years

ago when, at the age of fifteen, she dislocated her knee doing a spontaneous pirouette on the stone floor of her convent
school. The nuns gave her two aspirin and not much else. That
one carefree teenage dance step threw her hip and back out of
alignment. A doctor at Johns Hopkins agreed to do two hip replacements to relieve her pain, even though she was only in her
forties. In the end, she had no fewer than six operations for the
arthritis in her hips and her back: four hip replacements, a knee
replacement, and a spinal fusion in her early seventies. After
the fusion, she was never again able to straighten her spine, and
for the last fifteen years of her life, she has been forced to walk
with crutches to keep her body from tipping forward.

She doesn't complain. She simply carries on. The most we
ever hear is a gentle whooshing sound, an exhalation of pain
mixed with relief as she lowers herself into a chair. Until the
last few years, she drove everywhere, held down a full-time
job, did aerobic pool exercises to stay as toned as possible, and
when that became too difficult, she hired a trainer to come to
the house.

How do I justify weaning her off the painkillers when reports come in that she lies in bed sleepless, unable to get comfortable? I've emailed her doctor on vacation in Italy to ask for
another kind of medication that will ease the pain. I've told
Zuni to add a sleeping pill to the little pile of meds adminis-
tered at dinnertime.

Perhaps now she regrets asking me to be her "plug puller,"
the person responsible for medical decisions at the end of her
life. I'm the one who's worked the hardest on recovering from
living with her when she drank, so I'm the one most allergic to
the idea that she's reliant on substances of any kind.

THE CROSSING

DECEMBER 12, 1944–JANUARY 4, 1945

After losing the baby, my mother returned from two weeks of rest in the country to find a parcel of the underclothes my father had ordered for her from America. She wrote to her mother-in-law that everything fit perfectly, and that she had also mended Stewart's clothes, which were in a ratty state. Only a few more socks to darn and then all will be ready for his return. And then, in the third week of October, he did return. Sent by the OSS headquarters in Paris to demand more supplies for the Maquis, he flew over the Channel and landed in London with no time to warn anybody. The city—back in a party mood now that the buzz bombs had almost stopped—was more crowded than ever, so my parents were forced to hole up in a dreary little hotel, about the level of a bordello.

His leave only lasted a little over two weeks, but when he took off again on November 2 for France, he promised that this time it would be short. He just needed to make sure that his Maquis unit was properly resupplied, and then his mission would be complete. By the time he returned, only three weeks later true to his word, she told him she was pregnant for a second time. As my father mused in a letter home, if these first five months of marriage are any criterion, it looks as if *we'll end up with somewhere between thirty and forty children.*

British quarantine rules during the war decreed that if a woman did not leave the country before she was four months pregnant, she was required to stay until the baby turned two. My parents knew they were going to settle in America, and with my mother's continued anemia, the health of the baby was of grave concern. It was imperative that she get to the States as soon as possible so that her in-laws could fatten her up and give her a true respite from the years of rations and bombings. But she'd be traveling alone. Although his mission with the Maquis was finished, Stewart was still an officer with the OSS, waiting to see where he would be sent next. China was the most likely assignment.

When the newlyweds consulted the doctor about Tish's imminent departure, he was extremely reluctant to sign off on a transatlantic voyage, especially since his patient had suffered a miscarriage only three months before. Stewart pulled what strings he could to get her a seat on the Pan Am Clipper that had begun to make weekly flights over the Atlantic, but all transport for wives of American servicemen had been halted for the foreseeable future. It was through my grandfather's connections in merchant shipping that they secured a berth for her on the *Darro*, a refrigerated cargo ship of the Royal Mail line with room for a limited number of passengers. The doctor warned that she might well lose the baby during the crossing, but there was no other solution.

My mother was never given much advance notice when confronted with enormous changes in her life. She was pulled out of boarding school, evacuated from Gibraltar and married, all with little time to prepare. On Tuesday, December 12, the news came that the *Darro* was scheduled to depart from Tilbury Port the following Saturday. She had four days to pack up her life and say goodbye to her friends, her family, and her new husband. The *Darro* would be crossing the North Atlantic in convoy as the German U-boats were back in action, thanks to the invention of the periscope.

Every time I marvel at what she endured in those years, she shrugs it off, refusing to let me make her out as any kind of hero. "It was wartime. We had no choice. People went through much worse. When you're that young, you feel immortal, that nothing bad could happen to you."

I don't care what she says. I don't think I could have done it.

My mother and her father reported to the passport office, luckily run by an old English friend of Joe's, so she went to the front of the line. Her last passport, issued March 29, 1940, showed a wide-eyed girl in pigtails and a striped shirt, so clearly, she would need a new photograph.

In this one, a woman stares directly at the camera without the hint of a smile. The photo strips away my romantic ideas of my teenage mother, madly in love with her Yankee soldier, larking about London, dodging bombs, and ferreting out spies. She wears dark lipstick but no jewelry. The pigtails have been replaced with a cloud of unruly hair. In four years, she's grown into a married woman, pregnant for the second time, and headed across the ocean to a country where she knows no one. Her expression is wary and resigned. What will come, will come.

Tish's 1944 Passport Photo

When she handed her expired passport across the desk to the official in charge, the man burst into laughter at the photo of the pigtailed fourteen year old.

"By law," he told her, "I'm required to take this from you because if it falls into the wrong hands, the information can be used for a spy's false papers. But I'm going to let you keep it. This is something your grandchildren should see."

She thanked him politely and tucked the blue book into her luggage, which is why I found it six decades later in a file in her desk labeled IMPORTANT DOCUMENTS. The tired, withdrawn woman is the one I knew as a child. The wide-eyed girl in pigtails and a striped shirt is the one I've been searching for ever since.

With no warning siren, the first V-2, the most advanced pilotless rocket, hit Chiswick in South London on September 8, 1944, just as Londoners were rejoicing that the V-1s had come to an end because Allied forces had overrun the German launching sites in western France. Each V-2 rocket, weighing thirteen tons and smashing into the ground at the speed of three thousand miles per hour, created wide devastation. By early November, Churchill had to admit publicly that England was once more under attack.

When Tish stood at the railing of the *Darro*, looking down at the small collection of loved ones she was leaving behind, all she could think about were the V-2s. Now that it looked as if the war was finally coming to an end, would her husband, parents, and Bee survive Hitler's newest weapon? She mulled over that possibility for the ten days that the *Darro* was stuck in a pea-soup fog in the Thames estuary. The captain didn't dare move for fear of missing the channel and triggering one of the mines the British had dropped to keep the U boats from finding their way up to London. Everyone onboard could hear the whine of the V-2s over their heads, and the distant muffled explosions. When the fog finally lifted, the *Darro* steamed out of the estuary, and hugging the coast, made Southampton Harbor by Christmas Eve, just in time to join the convoy, a fleet of twenty-six merchant ships guarded by five escorts.

Because of their time in the Thames and the convoy's erratic course, Tish spent over three weeks on the *Darro,* where the passengers and crew celebrated Christmas and New Year's together. There was plenty of food, and even though she was in the first trimester of her pregnancy and traveling through the North Atlantic in the worst of the winter storms, she didn't get seasick. There hadn't been enough wood left in England in the fourth year of the war to finish the ship's deck, so the metal planking, constantly doused by ocean water, made it too dangerous for anybody to venture outside. As Tish spent most of her time playing the card game "hearts" in the common room with an American passenger who claimed to know the Alsops, she didn't remember her seven cabin mates very well, except for the four-year-old boy who slept with his mother in the bunk below hers.

Years later, when my oldest brother suffered a stroke in his late twenties, the doctors queried him about any unusual circumstances when he was in utero.

It was only then that Mummy remembered she had contracted German measles during the crossing, a very serious ailment for a pregnant woman in her first trimester. "It wasn't a very bad case, but I must have caught it from that little boy," she said to Joe on the phone.

Telegrams in code flew back and forth from London to Avon, Connecticut, so that when my mother disembarked in New York—first in line now that her last name began with the letter A—she was greeted by her mother-in-law, Corinne, and two dear friends she'd brought with her to the dock.

The trio of experienced New York ladies managed to find the luggage, hail a taxi, and escort this tired, shy, pregnant eighteen-year-old to lunch at the Colony Club, the Park Avenue home away from home for upper-class New York women. My mother, accustomed to unheated London flats—and more recently, the breezy common room on the ship—was dressed in "woolies" from neck to ankle. Soon after the little party was seated in the dining room for lunch, and Corinne's friends had begun to drop by the table to be introduced to Stewart's English bride, my mother slid to the floor in a faint. The overheated rooms, combined with the pregnancy, the long underwear, and a crowd of eager new faces had proven too much for her. Someone produced smelling salts, another lady fanned her with the printed lunch menu, and she woke to a circle of worried faces peering down at her from under their fancy hats.

The formidable Mrs. Alsop waited until the dessert course to break the most important news of all: my father had gotten himself a place on the *Queen Elizabeth*, an ocean liner which had been converted to a troop ship and which could make the transatlantic crossing in four days. He'd actually arrived in New York Harbor the day before. My mother had spent nineteen days on the ocean in convoy, while he sped over in a passenger liner, one of the many the Allies requisitioned for troop ships because they could outrun the U-boats.

My uncle John had convinced "Wild Bill" Donovan, the chief of the OSS, to bring Daddy back to the States and allow John to parachute into China in his place. So as soon as my father's ship docked, he left immediately to meet with Donovan in Washington. While my mother was taken off to Henri Bendels for a little shopping spree, my father and John lunched together in Union Station before Daddy took the train north to New York and John headed south to Miami to start his long trip to China. It would be eight months before they met again.

My parents spent their first night together in America in an apartment on East Sixty-Sixth Street that belonged to Helen Roosevelt, a cousin of my grandmother's. I don't know the address of the apartment or how the key was exchanged—or, more likely, as is the New York custom, left with the doorman. I don't know whether my father got there first and opened the door for my mother or the other way around.

My father, dead for over forty years, can't give me details. And if I'd asked when he was alive, he would have told me it was none of my business. My mother would look at me quizzically from her chair in the garden room, trying to follow me back into her memory bank: It's New York, Mummy. January 4, 1945. You had lunch with Grandmother at the Colony Club, and Daddy came up on the train from Washington. You met at Cousin Helen's apartment. Do you remember?

I won't ask. I'll leave them there, the two people who would in three years become my parents.

PART II

Early Marriage

Washington, DC
1945–1947

In a matter of weeks, my mother went from a fully employed decoding agent for the British Secret Service to a pregnant American housewife, bunking in with her husband's sister and family in the Georgetown section of Washington, DC. The house was small, the three children noisy, and her new husband preoccupied and increasingly nervous about how he was going to support a wife and a child. But there is nothing as lovely as a Washington spring, and she must have been grateful that she no longer had to cock her ear to the familiar whine of an incoming V-1, and that she could buy stockings for a song in the department store on nearby M Street. Soon enough, they moved to their own rental house on Twenty-Sixth Street, crammed into a row of others in what was considered a less desirable part of Georgetown. But again, she was no longer tiptoeing into the flat on the top floor at 60 Pont Street so her parents wouldn't hear how late she was getting home. She wasn't skipping across roofs collecting shrapnel or eating the miserable vegetables that wartime rations allowed. Thrilled with the supermarket bounty, she threw herself into cooking and learning her way around Washington—both the geography of the capital city and the intricate layers of its social scene—while waiting out the increasingly steamy days for her baby to be born. In March, when she was five months pregnant, she and Stewart were invited to lunch at the White House with the first lady of the United States, Eleanor Roosevelt. The president stopped by to say hello to his wife's relatives on his way to another meeting. At that moment, despite her parents' dismissal of her Yankee husband, it must have finally dawned on Tish that the Alsops weren't your run-of-the-mill Americans. One month later, the president was dead.

My father and Tom Braden, his fellow subaltern in the Kings Royal Rifle Corps, had convinced "Wild Bill" Donovan that they should write a history of the OSS. Donovan could be fierce, but to their surprise, he swiftly approved the project as, with the war winding down, he was fighting to convince the new United States President, Harry Truman, that the OSS should continue to be funded in peacetime. Donovan figured this book might bring some reluctant congressmen over to his point of view. So, while my mother cooked their meals in the small hot kitchen, the two buddies lurked about in the back rooms of the rental house, alternately arguing and typing.

When my brother Joe was born in late July, Tom—who would later father eight children and write a best-selling book about them called *Eight is Enough*—peered through the glass window at the squawling baby in the hospital nursery and suggested to my proud father that maybe he could exchange this one for another better-looking model. Daddy was wise enough not to repeat that remark to my mother for several years, as she would certainly have thrown them both out of the house.

My uncle Joe returned from China in the fall of 1945, thrilled to meet his new sister-in-law and his two-month-old namesake. Ever since their years at Groton, Uncle Joe had acted as if it was his particular job to keep his two younger brothers in line, and Stewart—with his sloppy habits, his record of misdemeanors at Groton and Yale, and his wayward women—had worried Joe the most. So, when Uncle John wrote to Joe in China that Stew had landed "a real charmer" who was not only beautiful but competent and sure to manage Stew with great efficiency, Joe had repeatedly championed my mother's cause in his letters home to Avon. The night he arrived in Washington my mother had managed to convince the local butcher to provide her with a steak large enough for twenty. Joe threw his arms around her and presented her with an enormous emerald ring, procured for her on the black market in Hong Kong. The reunion lasted through the night.

The next morning, with everyone a little worse for wear, Joe informed Stewart that he'd convinced the *Herald Tribune* syndicate to renew his contract and resume the weekly column he'd been writing before the war—but this time, with Stewart as a writing partner. My father was both grateful for the opportunity and nervous at the prospect of working with his older brother. Uncle Joe could be mercurial and demanding, and he set a merciless pace when it came to writing, traveling, and entertaining. From the beginning, Joe made it clear that he would be the senior partner and would keep sixty percent of the profits. This meant that in the first year of their partnership, Stewart earned only $7,000 from the column, a meager sum even in those days, to support his family.

Americans were eager to read war stories, in particular my father's stories, much to everybody's surprise. The book he wrote with Braden, entitled *Sub Rosa: The OSS and American Espionage*, made the *New York Times* best-seller list. Besides the extra income from royalties, this gave my father some credibility as Joe's junior writing partner.

In January of 1946, with the help of a family loan, my parents bought a brick row house at 2720 Dumbarton Avenue, four blocks up the street from Uncle Joe's, where the two brothers set up their office. Despite the rabbit-warren quality of the small bedrooms upstairs, my mother was thrilled with the garden in the rear and the rickety structure by the back wall that they shored up and used as a guest room. Braden moved in with them and lived there, more or less permanently, while he and my father finished promoting *Sub Rosa*.

By the spring of 1946, my mother had been living in America for fifteen months. Her new brother-in-law, Percy Chubb— the husband of Stewart's older sister—had generously given the newlyweds their honeymoon in the London Ritz Hotel two years before. Now, he suggested that Tish might want a trip home to England to see her family. Once again, he offered to pay for it, and she gratefully accepted. She left her husband

and Tom Braden with a mercurial housekeeper named Mrs. Johnson, who'd been sent over from Gibraltar by Cecilia, and nine-month-old Joe in Avon under the care of Mrs. Johnson's twenty-year-old daughter, Pat. (Pat's time with my grandparents coincided with one of Eleanor Roosevelt's annual visits to her cousin Corinne's farmhouse in Connecticut, so Pat got to meet the former first lady.)

By that time, the Hankeys were living part of the time in a little house on a relative's property in Kent, so with all her charges settled, Tish took off from New York and landed in Hurn, a former Royal Airforce airport on the outskirts of Bournemouth. She was away for six weeks, and my father missed her terribly. He let Tom move into the main house and put another bachelor, a fellow named William Clark, into the little house at the end of the garden. Stewart reported that Clark mistakenly turned on the gas instead of the hot water, which caused the boiler to leak all night, almost drowning Clark. My father hated having to manage anything even as mundane as calling a plumber, and clearly, he'd already grown used to my efficient, nineteen-year-old mother arranging his life.

She celebrated her twentieth birthday with her parents in Pont Street, where St. Columba's—the bombed-out church across the street—looked the same as the day after the attack, and her parents were still vociferous on the laziness of the British working man, a class snobbishness that Tish noticed more now that she had been away. In his letters from Washington, Stewart teased her that the Avon grandparents reported that little Joe looked *less like a small, cheerful, grinning little yellow old man, and more like a baby.* The day before she was due to come home, he wrote that two birds were making violent love on the lawn outside which made him jealous, as it was high time she was back in his bed.

So it was probably no surprise that by November, thanks to her strict adherence to Catholicism, my mother became pregnant for the third time. My father often laced his pronouncements with snippets of Shakespeare quotes, and he began to tell friends that the children were coming not "as the gentle rain from heaven" but as a mighty flood.

In January of 1947, with Stewart on an extended trip through the Mideast, Cecilia came from England to help out, crossing the Atlantic for what would be the first of many visits to America. Arthur and their two dogs stayed behind in the little house on his older sister's property in Kent, where the Hankeys had now moved permanently.

Tish was told to stay in bed as much as possible, as the baby was resting on a major artery, which meant that one of her legs was more or less permanently asleep. Every Monday morning, my grandmother would sit by my mother's bed and read her the weekly letter from Arthur. Usually, it went on about the weather, or the dogs, or the doings up at the big house which was occupied by his half-sister, Miriam, her companion Ann, and their pack of hunting dogs. But one morning in early April, the weekly letter informed my grandmother that her husband of twenty-eight years was leaving her for his wartime secretary. This was an irreversible decision, he declared, one that he had arrived at after much consideration. He would give her what monthly sum he could afford, but she was not to expect much. No apologies, no explanations. She was not to make any attempts to see him and would be allowed to communicate with him only through his solicitor. On both sides of my family, the habit has always been to convey distressing news, deep emotions, and uncomfortable feelings in writing, and preferably from a distance.

My mother was stunned. Did she think back to those months during the war when she and her father held down the fort at 60 Pont Street while her mother recovered from surgery down in the country? What secret assignations had he been keeping while she stayed out late, dancing in the nightclubs? No wonder he'd encouraged her to go ahead and have some fun now that Cecilia, their stern, humorless "housemother," was out of town. Earlier, when she was the only child still at home in Gibraltar, she and her father had spent many hours together riding along First River, the nearby Spanish beach. She'd crossed over to Morocco with him to watch a polo game. He'd made a photograph album just for her. But she couldn't forgive him for leaving her mother, and she never would. Although she would travel to England almost every year after she moved to America, my mother did not see her father again.

"Bloody coward," she muttered to me when I brought him up years later. "Imagine ending a marriage of almost thirty years with a letter like that."

Like many families with two children, theirs had paired off, and it shows in the family photographs. In one, the four of them are seated in a row on a stone wall. My ten-year-old mother is leaning against her father while they look through a photo album, her elbow planted comfortably on his upper thigh. The men are dressed in plus fours. Granny is knitting an enormous striped blanket, while laughing uproariously at a joke Ian has just told her. Ian was her favorite and Tish was his. After the dust of the war had settled, Ian and Arthur were gone for good, and the women were left with each other. It was never an easy relationship.

Ian, Cecilia, Arthur and Tish

Days after Arthur's letter, Cecilia traveled up to Avon to meet the other in-laws, a trip that had been scheduled months before. When she told Mrs. Alsop (or Mrs. A., as she was widely known) what Arthur had done, my father's mother flew into a fury.

"You must go home immediately and confront him," my Connecticut grandmother announced, and before Cecilia knew it, instead of returning to Washington, she was on a plane home, her resolve buoyed up by Corinne's outrage.

When she walked into their cottage in Kent, she found that Arthur had removed what furniture he thought was his. The dining room table remained, but the chairs were gone. Ghostly gray squares indicated which paintings he'd taken. Lamps were missing from tables, an entire collection of wedding china—which should, at least, have been half hers—was gone, and of course, all his clothes and personal belongings had been packed up and removed.

In a fury, she demanded that his solicitor release his current address, and the man, caught between two people, gave in to the one standing on his doorstep. Cecilia marched around to the bed-sitter, a small flat in public housing in a dreary London neighborhood. When Arthur answered the door, he was clearly stunned to find his wife on the other side of it. He thought he could count on the good Catholic woman he'd married to do what she was told. Granny never told my mother what she said to her husband that day, but she made it clear she would never grant him a divorce. Not long after, she packed up the house in Kent and shipped her belongings to Gibraltar, where her mother and sister gave her a floor in Marble House, her childhood home. Nobody ever mentioned her missing husband. Her friends and acquaintances acted as if she were a widow. She was known in Gibraltar as Señora Hankey, the lady in the black mantilla, who could be found most of the time at the Cathedral of St. Mary the Crowned, where she attended daily mass and served on the ladies' auxiliary. When her mother and older sister died, and the money petered out, my parents supported her. You can imagine my father's fury when years later, she informed them by mail that she had won the Gibraltar lottery of £30,000 but had given it all to the church. Until her last year, when my mother had to rush over to Gibraltar in the middle of my father's final illness to move her into a nursing home in England, Granny lived in Marble House.

I remember little about the few days I spent there when I was sixteen, except that I was free to roam the Rock on my own and that the galloping apes frightened me as much as they had my mother's maids. When Granny took me shopping downtown, I saw the black lace mantilla folded in her purse, always at the ready. The front foyer of Marble House was mercifully cool after the summer heat outside, the maids who cared for Granny were sweet and deferential although I spoke no Spanish, so we communicated in sign language, and Granny's focus on the church was absolute. She didn't seem that interested in me, and I was irritated that my mother had insisted I cut short my trip with friends in France to visit Gibraltar.

Now, thinking back on my teenage self-absorption and impatience, I feel sad for Granny. In seven years, because of the war, she lost everything. Her daughter married and moved across the ocean, her husband left her for his secretary, and the cruelest blow of all, her beloved only son was buried in a British military cemetery in Egypt. Ever since my mother handed me that manila folder with Ian's letters and papers, I've thought often about what it must have been like for my grandmother to open the front door at 60 Pont Street to the telegraph boy with the dreaded envelope lettered in black across the top, GOVERN-MENT ABSOLUTE PRIORITY.

The message was simple. DEEPLY REGRET TO INFORM YOU OF REPORT RECEIVED FROM MIDDLE EAST THAT 2ND LT I B HANKEY THE KINGS ROYAL RIFLE CORPS WAS KILLED IN ACTION ON 31 AUGUST 1942. THE ARMY COUNCIL DESIRE TO OFFER YOU THEIR SINCERE SYMPATHY —UNDER SECRETARY OF STATE OF WAR.

As the mother of a son, I cannot imagine recovering from news like this. Granny survived it all, clinging to her faith, to her routines, to her place in the British social circles in Gibraltar. Ironically, she lived two years longer than my own father.

The Third Child

1948–1949

By November of 1946, just eleven months after the launching of their column, "Matter of Fact" was running in fifty-seven newspapers across the country. It was clear that Stewart was carrying his share of the load. In setting up the partnership, Uncle Joe had insisted that six months of the year, one or the other of them would report from abroad. This was easy for him, a single man, but the constant traveling strained my parents' marriage. A year before, when my mother was dealing with her increasingly uncomfortable pregnancy, my father had spent the first three months of 1947 in Europe and the Middle East. His passport is covered with stamps showing him traveling in and out of London, Baghdad, Iran, Palestine, Egypt, Greece, Ankara, and Istanbul. His letters home from that trip were full of news of the stories he was researching, and although they ended with an *I love you* or *All my love*, he focused more on his constantly changing itinerary, which often depended on where brother Joe wanted him to go. If he felt any guilt about leaving his twenty-year-old bride for such long chunks of time, he comforted himself with the knowledge that Tish had learned to drive, and Cecilia came to Washington to help her daughter for most of the time that he was away. But as I look back now, I want to say to Daddy, *What the hell were you thinking?*

This is not the marriage my mother signed up for. It had been assumed that he would find some work that took him to an office every day, but what if she had known that he'd be traveling so much of the time, leaving her to hold down the fort with babies on the way and the people she hired who never seemed to stay? Of course, when they first got home after the war, he had no employment prospects at all, and once

Sub Rosa was finished, the future looked bleak until Uncle Joe came back from China with his proposal. When aspiring young newspapermen asked my father how to become a columnist, his answer always was, "Have a brother who is one."

But this was not an easy brother—so, caught between his need to prove himself to Joe and the demands of his burgeoning family, Stewart chose Joe and assumed that his efficient wife, young as she was, would cope as she'd always done. After all, not only had she been a decoding agent who'd survived in London during the war, but she was a British colonial, used to the long absences of family members.

And their marriage was a traditional one in that she tended the hearth and he served as provider. Daddy had great affection for us children and was always perfectly happy to hear there was another on the way, but he took no interest in our day-to-day affairs, assuming that Tish would take care of all that. In letters home, he referred to my older brother Joe as *little Ug* or *our mute son*, an arch way of keeping himself at a distance from baby concerns.

So, when Stewart announced that he'd be traveling to the Dominican Republic and Haiti in February of 1948, Tish convinced him that she should go too. After all, it was only a matter of weeks, and they'd be staying in the same hemisphere. He agreed. As my mother's period was always wildly irregular, they probably didn't know that she was already pregnant with me.

That summer, Uncle Joe wrote to his dear friend and future wife, Susan Mary Patten, that Tish was expecting *her third, slightly unwanted child*. Years later when I mentioned this comment to my oldest brother, he groaned in sympathy.

"Joe, face it," I said. "Mummy was a remarkably fertile woman and a Catholic. We were all slightly unwanted."

Of the seven children to whom my mother gave birth, I was the only child she didn't nurse. Because as a practicing Catholic she was only allowed to use what we called the rhythm method, she nursed Ian longer than any of us in the hopes that she could avoid another pregnancy. It didn't work. He and I were what people used to call Irish twins, born thirteen months apart. My mother at twenty two, had three children under the age of four. Desperate to get back some semblance of freedom, she handed me to a baby nurse with a bottle of formula.

When my father announced in early 1949 that he would be traveling for four months in the Far East to report on the post-war political climate in the former British colonies, she insisted on going with him, pointing out that she could arrange the travel and file his stories while he was interviewing sources. I expect they both thought it would put some romance back into the wartime marriage frayed by his travel, the stress of the journalistic partnership and on her side, the demands of three young children, and a social life that required constant evenings out and entertaining at home.

They left six-month-old me, my brother Joe, who was three, and Ian, who was not yet two, with my grandmother in Avon. The Butners, a mother and daughter from a displaced person's camp, were hired to help the regular staff—Aggie, my father's old nurse, and Emma, the cook. The Butners spoke German, Estonian, and Russian, but no English, so communication among those four must have been complicated. My mother was never good at hiring people, and letters from the early marriage often refer to housekeepers that aren't working out or pleas to my father on his trips abroad to ask friends where to find a nanny. With my Connecticut grandmother in charge, however, my parents took off as planned in late March and returned four months later, just in time for my older brothers' birthdays at the end of July.

My mother had booked them a passage by ship from California to Hawaii, which took three days. The girl raised on the shores of the Mediterranean was desperate for a touch of the warm ocean to erase the memory of her winter crossing of the Atlantic in 1944. Stewart prowled the deck like a caged lion, eager to get to the working part of the trip. They got so badly burned on the Hawaiian beaches that they had to coat

themselves with Vaseline in order to endure the long plane ride
to Tokyo.

Although my mother makes references to us in the ten letters she writes to her mother-in-law from the Far East, she is
more interested in impressing my grandmother with her newly
acquired knowledge of the shifting post-war politics in the re-
gion, so she chats on about the dullness of the Dutch in Bat-
avia, or the indignity of not being able to take a Japanese man
into a bar in Hong Kong. In an early letter from Tokyo, she
does say she longs to see the children and can't bear to think
about the changes she's missing. From Hong Kong, she writes
that she hopes the Butners are doing enough, that she doesn't
want Aggie and Emma to get tired. She sends two pairs of
rompers for me from the Raffles Hotel in Singapore, with the
instructions that they must be washed before I wear them. She
adds, *I long to see a picture of Elizabeth. I hope her hair has grown.*

Growing up as she did in a British colonial household where
any sign of emotion was discouraged, her lack of sentiment
isn't surprising. Children were raised by nannies and lived much
of their lives away from their parents. Her brother Ian was
shipped off to boarding school at the age of eight. At nine, he
sailed alone from Gibraltar to Plymouth, England, on a Union
Pacific passenger ship carrying boys his age from as far away as
Australia. When their cousin John traveled every August from
his father's tea plantation in Ceylon to an English boarding
school, he often didn't see his parents until the following June.

I can't imagine leaving my own children at that age for four
days, never mind four months. But my mother knew we were
well-cared for, and she grabbed at the chance to travel herself,
off on a lark with her handsome husband.

In early June, they made a detour to Kuala Lumpur to stay
with Henry Gurney, the high commissioner to Malaya, who had
been a Kings Royal Rifle Corps officer in North Africa during
the war. The occasion was the celebration of King George VI's
birthday, but the weather was so hot that the parade had to be
held at six in the morning. That night, Tish woke at two o'clock

in the morning to find her husband slipping out to join the jungle night patrol, hunting down Malayan insurgents.

"Are you mad? You're a husband and the father of three children. The patrols are dangerous. Why in hell are you doing this?"

"It will make good copy," he muttered and left the room before she could raise any more objections.

He came home safe and sound, but when they parted in Calcutta two days later as had been planned, she was still furious with him. (And with reason—two years later, High Commissioner Gurney was killed in an ambush by communist insurgents while patrolling in the jungle.)

From Calcutta, my father flew to Delhi while my mother started a three-day trip to Gibraltar, changing planes in Bombay, Rome, and Madrid. This was her first trip back to Gibraltar since the family had been evacuated in May of 1940. She'd left as a pigtailed girl of fourteen and returned as a twenty-three-year-old wife and mother of three.

As she reported in a letter to my grandmother in Avon, she had a wonderful time, motoring up to Granada past oxen plowing the fields, her face turned up to the hot sun. Granada had always seemed to her a Moorish dream, with the fountains playing in the Generalife, the palace gardens of the Alhambra, the oleander and roses in bloom, the oranges ripening on the trees, and the magnolias in full riotous flower. Although the place and the people had changed in her nine-year absence, things tasted the same, smelled the same, and the weather was glorious. Spain is still her favorite country in the world. She looked like a gypsy, all copper-colored, and wondered whether anybody back in America would even recognize her.

I'm the one who didn't.

❧

Five weeks later, my parents met up again in London, flew to New York, and made their way back to Avon to "retrieve" (my father's word) the children.

That summer day when the two world travelers walked up

the porch steps into the Avon kitchen, and called their hellos, the household was gathered, eager to greet them. Despite the confusion of people dropping bags and hugging, Aggie set me down because she wanted my parents to see that in the four months since they'd gone, I'd learned to walk. I toddled about quite confidently, eager as I was to keep up with my older brothers. I was dressed in the properly washed, pink seersucker rompers my mother had sent weeks ago from Singapore. Joe and Ian approached Mummy tentatively, but when she held her arms out to me, I ran crying back to Aggie, frightened of the copper-colored gypsy stranger who pretended to know me.

Our grandmother's house in Connecticut always felt like a safe haven to us three oldest children, and we looked forward to our visits at Christmastime and in the summer. In Avon, we were allowed to run free on the farm, but were supervised when necessary. In Washington, my older brothers and I counted on one another more than on the adults, as they seemed to be preoccupied with more important matters than raising a pack of children.

A nurturing mother would have made things better for all of us, but the boys at least grew up with a male role model in my father. My mother was the only other significant female in the house. I wonder now that if there'd been another woman in our lives—a constant presence such as Aggie was to my father and his siblings, or an older sister who could mediate and explain the world for me—I might not have missed Mummy so much or tried so hard to fit in with the boys.

To this day, the only photos of the two of us close together that I can find from my childhood were taken out at "Polecat Park," our nickname for the run-down farm in nearby Maryland where we spent most weekends and much of the summer. For an article my father wrote for the *Saturday Evening Post* entitled "Why Do I Keep the Damn Place?" the magazine sent one of their regular photographers to spend a day with us, and he set us up in various staged poses in order to record our daily life at Polecat. In one, he positions me in a baggy bathing suit, showing my mother a box turtle. We're in the dining room, and she admires my catch with a bemused smile, all the while looking like a high society version of a farmer girl in bare feet, a sundress, fancy earrings, and a rope of pearls around her neck. Three glum ancestors stare down at the unlikely scene from their gold frames. In another, my parents, Ian, and I are lined up on the porch, all of us looking to the left at something in the distance. I'm leaning against the arm of my mother's chair, with my feet up on a nearby column. It's a photograph I love probably because it paints a deceptive picture. My mother looks beautiful, calm, and benevolent, while I smile happily, the back of my head brushing the cotton flowered skirt of her sundress. The skin of my arm touches the skin of her leg.

Ian, Elizabeth, Tish, and Stewart on the porch with young Stewart in the background
Credit: Photo © SEPS

It was rare for me to hover that close to her for any length of time, as a clinging child made her restless and impatient.

Covert Ops

1950s

I grew up in a family of spies. My father worked for the Office of Special Services, my mother for the British Intelligence Service. Since they were forbidden to talk about their wartime activities, they kept secrets from one another from the day they met. It became a habit that morphed from the political to the personal.

By the early 1950s, my parents, affectionately known as Stew and Tish, lived at the center of glamorous post-war Washington DC, part of what was known as the "Georgetown Set." This referred to the people, who began after the war, to buy up housing in the oldest section of Washington. This square mile area, which for the last hundred years had been a slum, remained a strange mishmash of handsome, recently restored brick houses, factories, a government heating plant, and rickety shacks with outdoor toilets.

Ambassadors and diplomats and members of the Cabinet came to our house for dinner. My parents' closest friends either ran most of the CIA's covert operations during the 1950s and 60s or worked in the State Department helping to cover the spies' tracks—or, like my father and uncle, worked as journalists who were often debriefed by the CIA when they returned from abroad. Couples like Bob and Jane Joyce, Frank and Polly Wisner, and Desmond and Barbara Fitzgerald were in and out of our house all the time. Dick and Annie Bissell were regular weekend visitors to Polecat Park. My father played squash with Kermit Roosevelt at least once a week in the winter. Fourth of July weekend we usually went to Paul Nitze's farm, where Mr. Nitze engineered a fantastic firework display by the banks of the Potomac River. My brother Ian and I stayed with the

Braden family in Oceanside, California, while our parents attended the 1960 Democratic National Convention. At dancing school, I did turns around the floor with Tracy Barnes, David Bruce, Charley Bohlen, or Al Gore. Pictures from my debutante party show most of these kids as well as Lally Graham, Steve Schlesinger, and many others from "The Georgetown Set." In later years, my mother played weekly bridge with Kay Graham.

Dick Bissell, Des Fitzgerald, Kim Roosevelt, Tracy Barnes, and Tom Braden all worked for the CIA. Braden went from spy work to California politics and then back to Washington as a journalist. Chip Bohlen was our ambassador to Moscow and later to France. Paul Nitze was secretary of the navy. Until he committed suicide in 1963, Phil Graham was the publisher of the *Washington Post* and *Newsweek*. Often when I came home from school, one or another of these men would be sitting in our living room talking in low tones with my father, who was scribbling in his notebook. Every Thursday night when Joe, Ian, and I had an early dinner with Uncle Joe in his house, he was always dressed for his own dinner out with members of this group of friends (and sources for the column) or others like them.

The Second World War united these people. Many of them had served with the OSS. Some of them—like Tracy Barnes, my father, and Uncle John—dropped into France weeks after D-Day to liaise with the French resistance. Frank Wisner was stationed in Turkey and Romania. Des Fitzgerald fought in the Far East in the drive to retake Burma. David Bruce was head of OSS in London, and Bob Joyce was the OSS chief in Italy. They all had what my father called "good wars." Nobody was wounded, and they came home bursting with pride at what they'd achieved. They were patriotic and devoutly anti-communist. Not long after they returned to their pre-war jobs as lawyers or editors or administrators, they got restless and one by one, they gravitated to Washington, where the talk was always political, be it over a candlelit meal or a tennis net. Information was exchanged, sources were consulted, secrets divulged.

I'm not pretending that we children understood what was discussed or exposed. What we picked up was the atmosphere. It was as if we lived at the bottom of the ocean and, up above, shadowy boats moved back and forth through the murky water. Dark vessels maintaining radio silence. We heard an occasional ping from a hull, the steady thrumming of an engine, the turn of propellers. Where were they going? What were they looking for? Who was the enemy?

જે

When my brother Ian was told at the age of thirteen months that his new sister was named Elizabeth, he couldn't get his tongue around all four syllables, and came out with "Fuff." For a while my father, who loved to make up nicknames, called me "Fuffleberry Much." In the family the name stuck and in tenth grade, my first year at boarding school, I shed the "Liz" of my middle school years and introduced myself as Fuff. (One year, straight out of a page of the *Preppy Handbook,* I roomed with a girl named Muff.) In any case, it's a name people don't forget. When you call on the phone, you don't have to give a last name. Nobody ever asks, *Fuff who?*

In the row house on Dumbarton Avenue where we lived until I was six, Joe, Ian, and I slept in bunk beds in the nursery on the third floor. Stewart, the fourth child, born in 1952, spent the first year of his life in a tiny crib in a closet. When he got big enough to crawl out, we moved to the Cleveland Park section of Washington into a big, old rambling house circled by a crumbling driveway and a full acre of wooded land.

For children who had been limited to Montrose Park and the sidewalks of Georgetown, this place was heaven. After my early years in the nursery, sleeping in bunk beds with my two older brothers, I was happy to get my own room with a door I could close and a closet I didn't have to share. Still, at bedtime, I missed the companionship of the boys, even their teasing, and the way they planted their feet under my top bunk mattress and catapulted me into the air with no warning. This new house was huge, and the creaks from the boards at night and from the maids' rooms above my head made me a wary sleeper, attentive to each new sound.

Directly above the living room, we four children took possession of a playroom with its own fireplace in the western wall and a Zenith wooden console radio where we listened to *The Lone Ranger* on Monday nights. This room, as wide as the house and twenty feet long, became our exclusive domain. Sadly, the arrangement lasted only until my parents turned it into their bedroom wing, which must have been their plan all along. The space was large enough to fit a master bedroom, two dressing rooms, a bathroom, and a long hallway, all of it separated from the rest of the house by a very firmly closed door. The message was clear: private. All those who enter here better have permission.

Other than the midweek day that she drove the carpool to my convent school in Maryland, my mother rarely got up early. The maid of the moment made breakfast, we dressed ourselves, and often, legend has it, I dressed Ian as he was too lazy to do it himself. We trudged out the driveway to be picked up by the school bus or carpool, until the boys were old enough to bike the ten blocks to their nearby private school.

My parents' friends knew not to call them before ten o'clock in the morning. If the phone ever rang early in the morning, it meant the call was important, not from someone you could tell to try again later. It might be a source for Daddy's current column or a diplomat or even the White House. Whichever one of us picked up the phone would cover the receiver while we argued in fierce whispers about who would deliver the message. We knew the caller couldn't be kept on hold forever, so inevitably one of us caved in and went to hammer on the door that barred us from that forbidden hallway.

"Daddy?"

No answer. Open the hallway door.

"Daddy?" This time much louder.

"What?" His voice is faint.

"There's a phone call for you."

"I can't hear you." He opens their bedroom door.

"What is it?" he roars.

"A phone call for you."

"Who is it?" My mother's sleepy voice.

"I don't know. I think it's important."

"All right." Their bedroom door closes again.

Mission accomplished. The messenger tiptoes away.

The central part of the house we moved to in 1953 had been constructed in the nineteenth century as the farmhouse for a country manor on the other side of Springland Lane, our dead-end street. Gradually different owners tacked on two expansive wings to the original house so that by the time we took it over in the 1950s, it had tripled in size and spread in different directions. The connections between the oldest section and the new ones were so jerry-rigged that we could burrow into the bowels of the house like termites.

Because we grew up in a house filled with secrets both personal and national, none of which we understood, we became obsessed with digging out the truth. If we learned anything from our parents and their politically connected friends, it was that information gave you power. Although we were never clear about what exactly we were looking for, we adopted the tools of the spymasters who dined at our table and spoke with my father in the living room in urgent, lowered voices. We dug tunnels, we ran private phone lines through the sewers, we tapped bedrooms and dinner parties, and we taped conversations.

I remember very little about school; not the teacher's names (except for Mother Sessions, the terrifying nun who taught math in the sixth grade), not the classes or many of the names of classmates. In order to stay safe at home, I needed to be counted as "one of the boys."

There were three separate communities in our house. Our parents, locked away in their secret adult lives. The maids, who slept in small attic rooms on the third floor and kept us fed and the laundry washed, and the house cleaned in a haphazard way. And us kids, who, because so many parts of the house were off limits to us, set up our own secret headquarters in the basement.

When Joe suggested to Daddy that we children should be given the basement in exchange for our playroom upstairs, my father agreed, probably because it was the part of the house farthest away from his home office. The three rooms that Joe appropriated became our headquarters, and every day after school, Ian and I drifted downstairs, to stand at Joe's elbow while he fiddled with his electrical equipment or mixed up explosive chemical concoctions. We were perfectly happy to have him order us around. It gave us a focus, a way of blotting out the heavy silence that seemed to leak out of our parents' bedroom like an invisible poisonous gas.

Joe was our natural leader, not just because he was the oldest, but because he was a mathematical genius who came up with the kind of anti-grown-up schemes that occupied our time and gave us a sense of triumph over the opposing forces. He was the one who bet my father fifty dollars that he could bug the dining room during a dinner party without being detected.

Ian and I helped him run wire under the rug and handed him the small microphone when he was ready to attach it to the leg of the table by my father's chair.

The next evening, in that slice of time between Daddy's tennis game and my parents' dinner, Joe carried the heavy Wollensak reel-to-reel tape recorder into the living room. He set it up on the rickety table next to Daddy's special chair while Ian and I gathered around.

Daddy looked up from his book.

"What's this?" he asked.

By way of an answer, Joe pressed the play button, and the room was filled with the buzz of a Washington dinner party. We hadn't managed to get any state secrets on tape. To be honest, it was hard to hear what people were saying over the clink of the silverware against the china plates, but you could pick out familiar voices and an occasional phrase.

Daddy shook his head in disbelief, dug the silver money clip out of the pocket of his dinner jacket, and peeled off five tens. Joe took them without a word.

છે

My mother never paid much attention to our comings and goings, but she could be surprisingly accommodating the few times we turned to her for help. The fifty dollars disappeared quickly. To carry out his schemes, Joe often needed money.

Long before recycling became popular, Joe discovered that a junk place down in Georgetown—on the other side of M Street, near the canal—would pay you for old newspapers. The neighbors were happy to have us collect their newspapers twice a week. We picked them up in a red wagon and stored them in a great messy pile against the back wall of our garage. The weeks passed, the pile grew, and finally, it came time to deliver them and collect our money.

We asked Mummy to drive the station wagon down to M Street with our load. "Somebody wants to buy old newspapers? How bizarre."

"They're only open on Saturday afternoons," Joe explained.

"Do they pay you?"

"A nickel a pound."

Mummy shrugged. "Why not?"

When the station wagon was completely full and had sunk a good four inches closer to the ground, Mummy got behind the wheel, and with all of us stuffed into the front seat we headed for the recycling place down by the canal on M Street.

When we pulled through the gap in the large wrought-iron fence, a guard peered into the back of the car and waved us over to the scale. The system was simple. They weighed the car, we emptied it, and they weighed the car again. When the man tried to hand my mother the money, she nodded at Joe.

"It's his," she said.

Joe pocketed the bundle of rolled up dollars with a grin. We were in business.

Mummy never asked why we needed the money or what we spent it on. She had her own secrets. She let us keep ours.

FAMILY SECRETS

1957–1960

In those years, before my older two brothers left for boarding school, I felt safest in their company. Joe became our downstairs father, and I stood in his shadow and carried out his orders, no matter what they required of me.

One spring, we ran a secret telephone line from our house up to Rich Bissell's five blocks away on Newark Street. Mr. Bissell, the CIA operative responsible for the U-2 spy plane and later, the disastrous invasion at the Bay of Pigs, had been at boarding school with my uncle Joe and had grown up in Connecticut, where the families were friends. The Bissells spent lots of weekends at Polecat, our place in Maryland. Mr. Bissell always wore black Ked sneakers and black socks with his flappy, khaki shorts. He snorted loudly instead of blowing his nose into a handkerchief as we'd been taught to do. Mrs. Bissell was my mother's best friend. She had dark hair held back by a headband, and she dressed in wraparound skirts with flowers that looked as if they were made from slipcover material for a couch. In a commanding voice, she'd make odd pronouncements in short, elliptical phrases like some sort of double speak or code. I often didn't know what she was talking about, and I didn't feel safe with her.

Their oldest son, Rich, was Joe's best friend. Rich was tall and gangly. He had thick black hair and a big Adam's apple, and I didn't like the way he stared at me as if he were trying to see right inside my body. When Rich and Joe decided to run the wire through the storm sewers, I was selected to accompany Joe as I was the only one short enough to stand up in the culvert. Joe lay on his back on a wheeled pallet, pushing himself along with his feet while I followed with the roll of wire. We spent a couple of hours attaching the thick wire to the damp, curved walls, while dodging the occasional body of a dead rat and the pale green slugs whose bodies were suctioned to the ceiling.

It turned out that Rich and Joe had miscalculated the path of the sewer. Instead of turning right at the end of our block and heading up to Newark Street where Rich lived, the sewer ran straight under Reno Road, so Joe and I came up through a manhole in the middle of a remote extension of Rock Creek Park. The boys went back to the drawing board and managed, in a week, to run the wires overland, down alleyways, and across streets, looping the wire from one tree to another.

Although my mother certainly didn't know that we'd been down in the storm sewers and never said a word about our telephone system, she's the one who would have been most impressed with the set up. After all, she'd had first-hand experience with "scrambling," and her own reasons for keeping her conversations secret.

Meanwhile, my father kept traveling and my mother kept having children. Sometimes they both went away at the same time, but rarely in the same direction. The year I turned seven, the four of us kids, now including three-year-old Stewart, spent the summer with our Avon grandmother while my father traveled to Russia for a month. In August, he met Mummy in England for a ceremony where the Americans who'd enlisted in the Kings Royal Rifle Corps were introduced to Queen Elizabeth. In the photograph, my mother is dressed in a simple black suit with pearls at her throat, an outfit almost identical to the queen's white dress. She looks slim, calm, and chic, her white-gloved hands folded in front of her. You can tell that the queen is speaking directly to her; other people in the line are leaning out to listen, and although the queen is smiling brightly, my mother looks solemn and attentive, but not overly impressed. She's British, after all, and unlike the Americans on either side of her, she is at ease with the idea of royalty. Born only a month apart, these two young mothers, with their identical hemlines, two-inch heels, and pins on their lapels, look as if they could easily have been friends. (I used to tell people that my mother had named me after the queen, but it wasn't true. I was named after my great-grandmother, Elizabeth Winthrop Beach Alsop, because I was born the same day 101 years later.)

The American officers in the Kings Royal Rifle Corps meeting Queen Elizabeth in 1956. Tish in white gloves

My letter from Avon that summer assures my parents that I'm having a good time, that Stewart can't come to the pond because he doesn't know how to swim, and that Ian wants to buy a calf. In an aside, I mention that Grandmother is coming home in four days, so once again, it's clear that Aggie and Emma are in charge.

The timing of my father's trips had nothing to do with the situation at home. He went when some political crisis demanded his close attention, and it never occurred to him or to my mother to question that priority. After all, this was his job. This paid the bills. The home front was my mother's problem.

When he left on a trip, Granny came to stay. She and my father couldn't bear one another so they never spent more than one night in the house together. On some level, my British grandmother had never gotten over the fact that Daddy actually was a Yank, a member of a lower-class species who hadn't attended Eton. Although Mummy never said anything to me, I think she also dreaded these visits. Granny could be critical of everything: our table manners, the dusty bookshelves, the slovenly kitchen staff. She went with us to Saturday Confession and Sunday Mass, wearing her black lace mantilla, looking like a grandmother from another century. I was always relieved when it was time for her to go home and I think my mother was too. With Granny in the house, it was harder for Mummy to hide her drinking, which by now had developed into a furtive, daily habit.

After one especially long trip, I made a four-foot, crepe paper "Welcome Home" banner for Daddy that I hung over the fireplace. My younger brother Stewart and I stationed ourselves at the living room door so we could see his reaction. My mother was moving restlessly around the room, straightening the pillows on the sofa, and adjusting the curtains.

"He's here," I shouted the moment the airport taxi turned the corner at the end of the driveway.

My mother whirled around.

"Both of you, upstairs," she barked. "Right now,"

"But, Mummy, I want to see—" I cried, but she cut me off.

"Not another word. Off you go." We knew that voice. We didn't argue with it.

I got to the second-floor windows just in time to see her throw herself into my father's arms as he clambered out of the cab. I couldn't believe it. My mother and father were hugging each other. Their skin was touching. They were kissing.

Stewart, on his tiptoes, begged me to lift him, but when Daddy glanced up, I pulled us both down beneath the windowsill. Even with his arms around Mummy and his cheek buried in her hair, my father was scanning the house to see if anybody was watching.

❧

Because we lived in such separate communities, I don't

remember much about my mother's life in my growing up years. I know she was a very good cook, although she rarely made our meals. That was the maid's job. Uncle Joe insisted that she and Daddy entertain as much as he did because in those days in Washington that was one of the ways to interview their sources, who were as often as not, their friends. My mother was renowned for her cooking, so many nights I fell asleep to the rumble of voices intermingled with the clatter and clink of glasses in the dining room directly below my bedroom.

As the readership of my father's weekly column "Matter of Fact" continued to increase, my father began to gain as much fame as his older brother. In 1957, Uncle Joe took an extended trip abroad, so attention naturally shifted to his younger brother, holding down the fort on the domestic front. One spring night that year, when Edward R. Murrow brought his television show *Person to Person* to our house, we children were paraded downstairs dressed in our Sunday best so he could feature us in the program.

Ed Murrow was a friend of my father's. Their paths never actually crossed in London during the war, but they were aware of each other and connected once they both came home. In their column, my father and uncle denounced Senator Joe McCarthy in the early 1950s, and Murrow dealt the senator's reputation a deathly blow in a half-hour special report of his show *See It Now* that aired in March 1954. By the time he came to interview the Stewart Alsop family three years later, Murrow had invented the celebrity profile on television. Each episode of *Person to Person* was divided between serious interview subjects and entertainment celebrities. We were season four, episode twenty-six, and during the second half of the show, Murrow interviewed a New York bandleader named Ted "Is Everybody Happy?" Lewis. We counted as the serious segment.

Mr. Murrow was beamed in from the CBS studio in New York. A producer briefed my parents as to how the program would proceed and which questions Murrow wanted to ask. We were told to look at a camera that had been secured to a corner of the dining room and pretend we could see his face. Whenever the red light went on, his disembodied voice floated over our heads. Watching the tape now, it looks sloppy and amateurish. In the living room, Murrow asks my mother a question that she never answers and suddenly my father is introducing us in the dining room. We are lined up with our backs to the camera in imitation of generations of Alsop family photographs. When Daddy turns us around, the audience can see the older boys are dressed in jackets and ties. Joe's tie is neatly knotted while Ian's is already coming unraveled. I'm wearing a cotton dress with a white collar and a fat, flouncy skirt. Stewart is kitted out in shorts with attached suspenders.

At twelve years old, Joe stands up straight and greets the corner camera with a convincing, "How do you do, Mr. Murrow?"

Ian mumbles a bit, I say hello in a sure, strong voice, and Stewart, who has just turned five, gets out a "hi," after his tongue has completed one full circuit of his lips.

"Who's the budding writer in the younger set?" Murrow asks.

"I am," I announce without skipping a beat.

"What kind of things do you like to write?"

"Well, I like to write stories."

"What kind of stories?

"Well, sort of animal stories."

Ian talks about painting whales and Joe says he likes to "hack around with little electric motors and little bells and buzzers." We are standing directly above Joe's three basement workrooms where he hacks around with a lot more than little bells and buzzers.

As soon as we've had our moment in the spotlight, Ed suggests to my mother that with four children, she must have a very busy day. That's her cue to announce in her clipped English accent that we've been up very late, "so I think we'll say goodnight and push off to bed."

"What a wonderful family," Ed says as she herds us around the long dining room table adorned with a massive silver candelabra. As we exit stage left up the stairs, my father strolls down the hall to the living room, with Ed's voice still floating above him and a man pushing a rolling camera trailing along behind him.

"There seems to be considerably less gloom and doom in your household," Ed says to my father, "than in the columns you and your brother write."

By that time, we've been marched smartly up the stairs, although Mummy says we can stay up and listen as long as we don't get in the way while she returns to the living room for the rest of the interview.

For a shy thirty-year-old, she does pretty well in the spotlight, although her British-accented voice quavers a little as she's showing Murrow pictures from the family album and discussing her household duties.

That same year, the *Washington Post* published an article about her entitled "'Angel' Duty Keeps Her Flying from Pole Cat [sic] Park to Wards." Encouraged by her friend, Annie Bissell, my mother volunteered at the Washington Emergency Center as a ward secretary on Tuesdays and Thursdays. Besides helping the nurses with administrative duties, she often sat by patients' bedsides and wrote letters for them.

Mummy was the one you wanted by your side in a hospital. When a doctor decided that I, at the age of twenty-one, should have my tonsils out with a local anesthesia, it was my mother who noticed, as I was rolled out of the operating room, that I had passed out and was in danger of swallowing my tongue. She took our various injuries in stride, from the time Joe blew up his hand in the barn at Polecat to the time I sucked a large gold bobby pin down my throat through a straw.

"What in heaven's name were you trying to do?" she asked on our way to the hospital.

"Spit it at Ian," I admitted.

When it showed up on the x-ray in the emergency room, the doctor told us that we'd have to wait for it to "come through." She didn't blink an eye.

"A pretty, brown-eyed blonde," as the *Post* article described her, my mother did indeed look like an angel. That face combined with the British accent made patients and interviewers alike fall in love with her. She appeared to sail through her days juggling the two households, the demands of her husband's career, and her own volunteer work.

That was the outside. Inside, she was miserable. She'd never gotten over her natural shyness, but she learned early on that alcohol made all those formal Washington occasions so much easier. At some point, she drank too much at an embassy party and made a spectacle of herself. My father warned her that any public display like that must never happen again as it would jeopardize his reputation and certainly his job. So, she went undercover. This occurred early enough in their marriage that we children never saw her drink alcohol. While Daddy had his bourbon before dinner, wine with dinner, and one or two beers afterward, she drank Coca Cola. We didn't know there was vodka in the glass, which she used because it had no scent and was hard to detect. Daddy drank lots and his mood never seemed to change. It mystified us that Mummy seemed always on edge. Ian and I came to the conclusion that she had some form of mental illness. We tossed around words like "schizophrenic" and "depressive" without having any idea what we were talking about.

She was a chemical alcoholic and a binge drinker. This meant she could be off the sauce for a week and on for a year, or the other way around. We knew something was wrong if she was smoking because she only smoked when she was in that strange, tense mood. Other signs were less obvious. She had a habit of twirling a lock of hair between the first two fingers of her right hand, which must have been her way of relieving anxiety. Back and forth, back and forth, the blonde curl would go for what seemed like hours. I can replicate the movement now, all these years later, because it's so ingrained in my memory. When her fingers weren't twirling the hair, they were twitching by her side. Her voice took on a brittle edge and her responses to our questions were completely inconsistent.

On Tuesdays and Thursdays, she drove Annie Bissell to the

hospital, and one day, on the way home, Annie asked her in for a drink. My mother was shocked at first because in our house there was always that dictum about no cocktails until the sun had passed over the yardarm. Those secret afternoons in Annie's kitchen tipped her over the edge, and the drinking moved from pleasurable to necessary.

The worst times came when Daddy was traveling abroad, Mummy was locked upstairs in her bedroom, and the maids had disappeared to their two small rooms under the third-floor eaves. Those days, if we weren't hiding out in the basement, we children roamed around the house like ghosts.

But you could still count on her in a crisis.

We started digging the bomb shelter the same summer we lost Laddie, our favorite beagle. His death gave us an inkling of how quickly the world can spin, which may have inspired Joe to try to protect the family from whatever disasters the future held.

Daddy grew up on a farm where dogs were a given. We'd always heard that our grandfather preferred his dogs to his guests and, on occasion, his children. In Gibraltar, my mother's life was also full of dogs, beginning with a series of "stupid spaniels," as she called them, and ending with Romulus and Remus, the two corgis shot and buried at sea.

My older brothers agitated for dogs for some time before my mother finally relented and bought them two male beagle puppies from the same litter. Joe got Spotty who was pudgy and slow, but eager to please and had a bark that was more of a squeal. Laddie was Ian's. My favorite, he had brown ears, a thin white blaze above his dark eyes, and a sweet disposition. The beagles didn't really require much work—we just let them out the back door both in the city and the country. Sometimes it was hard to round them up on Sunday nights after a weekend at Polecat, where they tore around the fields, bellowing and chasing rabbits until their tongues hung out. Other than that slight inconvenience, they fit easily into our lives until one

summer weekend when we took them with us to a farmhouse
our friends the Bradens had rented somewhere in Virginia.

Early in the morning, when they were barking to get out,
someone opened the front door and the two tore across the
field, howling with delight at the tantalizing smells. The household rose in a leisurely fashion. If anybody heard gunshots, we
didn't mention it to one another. My father was standing on the
porch in his bathrobe when Spotty, squealing at a higher pitch
than usual, barreled back across the field, tail between his legs.
Ian and I came out to see what the matter was. A man was walking toward us, carrying something in front of him from what
looked like a long stick. The stick turned out to be a rifle shoved
through Laddie's collar. Bleeding from the chest, our brown
and white beagle was dangling from the gun barrel, swinging
from side to side in step with the man's stride.

He stomped up to the edge of the porch and jerked the gun
backwards so that Laddie's dead body dropped into the grass
at his feet.

"This dog killed two of my chickens," the man growled,
"Chased them till they dropped dead of heart attacks."

"You shouldn't have shot the dog," my father said. "I would
have paid for the chickens." I don't remember anger or threat
in my father's voice, just disbelief.

Without bothering to answer, the man turned on his heel
and started back toward his farm.

"Kill him, Daddy, kill him," Ian screamed, pounding on my
father's arm. "He shot Laddie. Shoot him."

Without a word, Daddy turned and went back into the house.

My mother took over. She wrapped Laddie in a towel and
sent Joe for a shovel. It was summer. We couldn't take a dead
dog home in the back of a hot station wagon. She supervised
the digging in a cool spot under the shade of an oak tree and
gently placed our sweet beagle in the hole, while Joe held the
whimpering Spotty by the collar before he could jump into the
grave with his brother. I was crying without making a sound,
Ian was staring into the hole in disbelief. My father stayed inside

the house with our hosts. Once we left, that was it. This was not a place we'd ever come back to.

Packed into the second seat of the aging station wagon, we usually argued most of the way home on Sunday nights until Daddy silenced us with a roar of frustration.

But the night we left Laddie's body behind in a shallow grave, nobody spoke for the entire ride home.

You could rely on my mother in a crisis. It was the times in between that she disappeared.

Later that summer, the last one before Joe left for boarding school, he decided we should dig a bomb shelter.

My father and uncle were convinced that President Eisenhower wasn't doing enough to close what they later termed the Missile Gap, so there was a lot of talk in our house about the Russians and their weapon systems and their trajectories. We children living in the nation's capitol knew perfectly well that if World War III started, our city would be the first target. It added a certain urgency to the country's discussion of drills and bomb shelters. Like other children in America, we learned to spot the yellow triangles on public buildings which indicated a safe place to shelter. But we also knew people who built personal bomb shelters. My uncle in Connecticut constructed a concrete room on the side of an old barn on his property. Years later it turned into a storage place for all the extra furniture and books that came out of my grandmother's house after she died. Up in Maine, one friend of my parents designed an elaborate bomb shelter with shelves for the canned goods and a locked cabinet for the guns he'd have to use to keep the desperate neighbors at bay, the ones who hadn't properly prepared the way he had.

My parents discussed the safest place for all of us to go should a nuclear attack appear imminent. One day, my father came home from his weekly squash game and announced to my mother that we were going to share the construction of a bomb shelter with Kermit and Polly Roosevelt. (Kermit, known as

Kim, was Theodore Roosevelt's grandson and a political action officer at the CIA who had engineered the overthrow of the democratically elected prime minister of Iran in 1953.) My father was especially thrilled with this idea because it meant they'd have a foursome for bridge, which he figured would help the hours pass more easily. My mother categorically refused. She found it difficult to get through a dinner party with Polly Roosevelt, never mind weeks trapped in a confined space. She had her own plan. She would take us children out to Polecat Park, and we'd live off the land for as long as it took. As she'd survived two years of bombings in London, she spoke with a certain authority and my father relented. If the dire predictions about the widespread nuclear holocaust proved true, then all their discussions were ridiculous. How could she possibly drive us out of the city when the roads would be choked with other escapees? Wouldn't the nuclear cloud extend as far as Polecat, fifty miles from the White House? What kind of warning would any of us have? No matter how close my father was to his sources in the CIA and the State Department, they probably wouldn't have time to spread the word to us ordinary citizens. This conversation continued over many months, and my parents' energy for the project waxed and waned depending on the news of the day.

As usual, Joe took matters into his own hands. If they weren't worried, well, he was. One summer morning, when our parents were both abroad and the maids were once more in charge, Joe hustled us out of bed with a command to meet at a site across the driveway from our front porch. He handed out shovels and told us to start digging.

Washington soil is mostly clay. It's reddish, dense, hard to cultivate, but excellent for maintaining the walls of a wide hole. What we discovered that first hot morning was that it's almost impossible to dig. After an hour of sweaty work, we'd barely made a dent in the ground. And since Joe decided the dirt shouldn't be allowed to pile up next to the hole, he made us carry it in buckets all the way down to the edge of our property nearest the street and then climb back up with the empty buckets. We quit before the morning was out, complaining that we spent more time delivering the dirt than we did digging. That night Joe invented a solution.

You filled a bucket at the top of the hill with dirt, hooked it onto a long, sturdy wire, and sent it racketing down the hill. At the bottom, it knocked into a tree branch that tipped the contents out onto the slope next to the stream. The weight of the downward bucket pulled the empty one back up. It was ingenious.

Word got around the neighborhood, and soon the kids from up and down the street were clamoring to use the bucket system. With our parents away, the maids fed us and washed our clothes and, probably with great relief, left us to our own devices, which was, of course, exactly what we wanted. We'd never have gotten away with the digging of the hole if Mummy and Daddy had been around. Even though they paid little attention to our various projects when they were home, this one was out in the open, only a few feet beyond the wall of the driveway that was used all day long for errands and deliveries. By the time Joe declared the shelter finished, we'd dug a fourteen-foot hole as well as a room at the bottom where he, Ian, and I spent one eerie night equipped with comic books, flashlights, and sleeping bags and surrounded by the tree roots.

That year, Daddy came home first while Mummy stayed in Gibraltar with her mother. When Joe invited him to tour the bomb shelter, my father was going through the mail. He looked up and made an effort to focus on us. We never expected him to remember our birthdays or what grade we were in, but sometimes I wondered if he even knew how many children he had. His mind was always elsewhere. But this time, with Mummy gone, he followed us out to the front driveway, figuring he would humor us with a brief visit to the "bomb shelter."

We three were standing at the top, when he climbed slowly back up the ladder.

"Where'd you put the dirt?" he asked.

"Down at the bottom of the hill," Joe said.

"You carried all that dirt?"

"We used this," Joe said, and released the top bucket. It rattled its way down and the empty bucket appeared as if by magic. Daddy shook his head in amazement. Where had this first son of his come from? "We haven't put in the shelves yet," Joe said quickly. "I'm working on that."

"Shelves?"

"For the supplies. They say you need a month of supplies in a bomb shelter."

Daddy nodded as if in agreement, but he didn't say anything more. Like a man in a dream, he clambered over the brick wall and marched up the stairs to the front porch.

"What did he think?" I asked.

Joe shrugged. "Who knows?"

It didn't take us long to find out.

The next day a crew of men arrived with a pile of lumber. As we watched in disbelief, they assembled a massive wood cover for our hole. When our father came home from work that night, Joe attacked.

"What's going on?"

"Your bomb shelter," Daddy began with just the slightest hint of sarcasm in his voice, "is dangerous. Because of it, I've had to increase the liability premium of our homeowner's insurance policy. Any kid could fall into it and not be able to get out. It could give way and suffocate the lot of you."

"But the cover is much too heavy for us to move," I cried. "We can't go down by ourselves."

"Precisely," my father said.

Joe turned away with a murderous look on his face.

I think my mother would have let us keep the hole. After all, she was the girl who skipped across the top of roofs to collect shrapnel and dragged furniture out of burning buildings. But by the time she got home, there was nothing to be done and she never openly defied my father. Instead, she instructed the people who raked leaves in the fall to put them down the hole. Slowly it filled up, even though you can still see a slight depression in the slope that marks the spot where fifty years ago, we dug the bomb shelter.

JULIE NIXON'S DOLL

1958

My older brothers provided me with a sense of safety, a wall between me and our parents' silent standoff, but one by one they began to leave. Joe was the first to go. The fall after the bomb shelter summer, following in a family tradition, he started at the Groton School in Massachusetts at the age of thirteen. My father, his brothers, my grandfather, and my great-uncle had all gone to Groton and from what I can tell, they all hated it. Years later, Daddy was surprised to learn that his sons expected anything else. Upon hearing their complaints about the place, he exclaimed in amazement, "But you're supposed to be miserable at Groton."

Meanwhile, the tensions in the house, always unspoken but detectable, increased. Two months before we appeared on *Person to Person*, my uncle Joe, who was a closeted homosexual, had been caught in a honey trap in Moscow and photographed by the KGB in bed with a man. His sexual adventuring posed a great threat not only to his job and livelihood, but to my father's. In those days, America in general, and the government in particular, was filled with fanatic homophobes. When my father started looking to sever his connection with their column and go out on his own, Uncle Joe, in a fit of pique, told him to see what he could find, clearly assuming his younger brother wouldn't be able to make it on his own. In the spring of 1958, Daddy was hired by the *Saturday Evening Post* as their Washington editor, which gave him the opportunity to write longer articles. His mandate was to explain the workings of the nation's capital to the rest of America. Uncle Joe was hurt and lashed out. Their arguments in front of the fireplace after dinner grew louder and more vehement, and for a while, the brothers saw less of one another.

Our father started working much of the time in his home office. When I came home from school to the pounding of keys on his old Underwood typewriter, I knew to stay away from the front of the house. Sometimes he could be found interviewing people in the living room. Other times, he would throw open the office door, stride into the living room, circle the couch and circle it again, rolling between his thumb and forefinger the gum he chewed to cut down on his cigarette habit. If he happened to encounter any of us children on the floor in the front hall, he'd step over our bodies as if we were nothing more than pieces of furniture briefly blocking his progress. Then he'd pop the gray wad of gum back in his mouth, and with a slam of the door, disappear once again into the office. If my mother needed him for something, she knew to call him on the phone from the living room to the office, a distance of twenty feet. Lost in whatever thought he was pursuing, he would materialize like a ghost in our midst and then melt away through the wall.

Even though my emotional memory tells me that I saw little of my mother when I was growing up, she did understand certain things about me. She knew, more than anyone else, that I needed to fit in with the boys. Except for important occasions like Sunday Mass, the official Christmas family photographs, or Washington society birthday parties, she let me wear Ian's cast-off pants, plaid shirts, and old sneakers. I looked as ragtag as I could and wore my clothes like a badge. It meant I could keep my footing when we scrambled over the roof between our bedrooms, or that I could go after crayfish in the stream without getting tangled up in skirts. It meant I could pass as "one of the boys."

I must have had girl friends in Beauvoir, my first school, but I don't remember them. Beauvoir was the private school of choice for the Washington elite, and since most of the mothers didn't work outside the home, the more socially connected of them threw their energies into organizing events for children.

In one photograph, I'm attending a Georgetown birthday party for Wendy, the daughter of Frank and Polly Wisner. She was a year older than I was, but because her parents were friends of mine, I'd been included. (Her father was at the height of his career as director of the Office of Policy Coordination at the CIA.) Bachrach, the society photographer at the time, took the official party picture, and I'm way in the back, dressed in a frilly white blouse and plaid kilt skirt held up by plaid suspenders. Like a mouse peeking out from a hole, my tiny solemn face, barely visible to the photographer, peers over the shoulders of two other children. A mother or governess on the floor in the front is arranging the strings and labels for an elaborate treasure hunt. Four parents, including my mother with too wide a smile, hover above us, and the only child who looks more miserable than me is Wendy herself. I don't think any of the children who attended were particular friends of hers or of each other. Even children's birthday parties in Washington could be used as an excuse for a repayment of political debts or an opportunity for an off-the-record interview.

So, looking back, I'm now not surprised that, at the age of nine, I was invited for a play date at Julie Nixon's house. The first long piece my father wrote for the *Saturday Evening Post* was an in-depth profile of the vice president of the United States, Richard Nixon. In those days, the vice president didn't live in the sumptuous estate on the grounds of the Naval Observatory on Massachusetts Avenue, but in a house he'd bought with his own money. In 1957, Nixon had moved his family into an eight-bedroom stone house on Forest Lane, overlooking Glover Park, a neighborhood not far from ours in Cleveland Park, but considered slightly less fancy. Daddy had prepared carefully for the first exclusive interview that Nixon had granted since he'd become vice president six years before, so his list of questions was long. He was invited to the Nixon's house, where his wife Pat Nixon welcomed him, served coffee on the porch for the two men, and then discreetly disappeared.

A few weeks later, she called my mother to invite me over to

play with Julie, who was only three months older. This phone
call was odd, as my parents were not social friends of the vice
president and his wife, and few people in Washington knew the
Nixons personally. Nixon distrusted the Georgetown set, and
they felt pretty much the same about him.

In a rare act of rebellion, I spoke up.

"I don't want to go to her house. I don't even know her."

"No choice," my mother said crisply.

"I'm not going to wear a dress," I said half-heartedly, wish-
ing she would make me.

"You don't have to," she said. "I'll wait for you in the car."

Daddy was in California continuing to research the Nixon
article, and my mother knew it would be a slap in Pat's face if
we turned down her invitation. Pat was doing her bit as the dutiful wife of the vice president to influence the tone of Daddy's
article, and my mother was going along with the charade.

At home on Springland Lane, my bedroom, although spa-
cious, looked no different than the boys' rooms. The furniture
was serviceable, the lights worked intermittently, the bureau
drawers stuck as I opened and closed them, and the venetian
blinds often hung at a peculiar angle as it was always hard to
coax the cords to move up and down in unison. The curtains,
sewed from leftover couch material, were rarely washed or replaced, no matter how dilapidated they got. At one point in
my teenage years, I did get a dressing table of sorts when my
mother moved it out of her dressing room to make room for
a larger one. In general, she concentrated on decorating the
main entertaining rooms, and as long as we children had beds
and serviceable plumbing, she didn't pay much attention. The
maids vacuumed once a week and changed the sheets. If our
rooms got too messy, my mother just closed the doors as she
passed by.

In contrast, Julie's bedroom in the Forest Lane house was
more typical of a girl's room of the late 1950s. The walls were
painted a pale blue, the delicate white curtains at the windows
had been made by her mother, and the room was full of dolls

and dollhouses. It was reported in the newspapers that she and her older sister Tricia had attended the inaugural ball earlier that year in short pink party dresses. When I had to wear a dress to church, it was usually one of those smocked numbers that my English grandmother sent over from Harrods. But Mummy had let me stay in Ian's hand-me-down shorts and plaid shirt, which made me appear rough and out of place in this feminine space. We two girls didn't know what to do with each other. By default, we played with dolls, and I counted the minutes until Mrs. Nixon finally called up the stairs to say that my mother would be coming soon to pick me up.

After a moment's hesitation, I picked up Julie's favorite doll and carried it downstairs while she followed behind, demanding its return.

In the kitchen, Mrs. Nixon smiled benevolently at me, while Julie complained that she wanted her doll back.

"Mrs. Nixon," I asked in my most polite party voice, "could I have this doll?"

Julie began to wail while her mother weighed her options.

"Of course, you can, Elizabeth," she said, shooting her daughter a look. "Julie, be quiet. Elizabeth is your guest. If she would like to keep this doll, then of course she can have it. You have lots of other dolls in your room."

"But that's my favorite one," Julie cried. And I knew it was. That's why I'd chosen it. Outside, I heard my mother beeping the horn. I curtsied and thanked Mrs. Nixon, ignoring Julie, who continued to howl in rage, and scooted out the door. I knew if my mother came into the house, I was sunk.

I jumped into the front seat, clutching my prize.

"Let's go," I said.

"Did you have a good time?"

I nodded.

"Did you say thank you?"

"Yup," I said. Time to go, Mummy. I was sure that any minute Julie would burst through their front door.

"What's that?" my mother asked, indicating the flouncily dressed lump in my lap.

"A doll," I said, stroking one of its plastic knees. "Julie gave it to me."

"That was sweet of her," she said. Then after a moment's pause, she added, "But you don't like dolls."

"I like this one." Please, please drive away now.

Finally, after one more long look at me, my mother put the car in gear, and we rolled slowly down Forest Lane away from the scene of the crime.

When I got home, I spirited the doll up to my room and hid it deep in the back of my closet where the boys wouldn't see it. I don't know what happened to it. I expect that in one of my mother's sudden fits of clearing out, it went out the door to the Catholic charity thrift shop.

Two months later, my father's article on Richard Nixon was published in the *Saturday Evening Post,* and although balanced, it presented a surprisingly positive picture of the man who was already sure to be the 1960 Republican candidate. Surprising mostly because, as my father admits in the beginning of the article, he was inclined to be disdainful and dismissive of Nixon as nothing more than "a shrewd, tough, ambitious politician."

Little did Pat Nixon know that my father had no concept of my daily life and my mother not much more. In any case, nothing good or bad that might have happened to me at the Nixon house would have changed one word of Daddy's *Saturday Evening Post* article. But somehow, without being told, nine-year-old me had divined an ulterior motive for my invitation, and I had parlayed that little slice of power and my resentment at being used into an act of outright thievery. I was angriest at the grown-ups: my mother for playing along and forcing me to go without insisting I wear a dress, Mrs. Nixon for suggesting the play date in the first place, and on a deeper, more unconscious level, my father for instigating the entire situation. Because I couldn't pay them back, Julie was the one who suffered. Stealing something you really want is one thing but stealing something you don't even want just to make another person miserable ranks much higher on the list of sins.

Near and Far

1950s

Roman Catholicism has had two important functions in my life. It gave me a pack of siblings, a crucial gift to a lonely child. And it gave me confession and mass, the two weekly church rituals when I knew Mummy would stay close by, no matter how badly we misbehaved or how much she wanted to slip out the side door and disappear, the way she so often did at home.

On the maternal side of my family, back through the generations, the Catholicism has come down through the women. Although my great-grandfather, Alexander Mosley, was raised a Protestant, he married a Spanish-Italian Catholic, Maria de la Mercedes Francia. Their daughter, my grandmother Cecilia, also married a British Protestant, and my mother married a New England agnostic who was raised in the Congregational Church.

Even though my father refused to convert to Catholicism, he agreed that we all could be raised Catholic—but he claimed the right to educate the boys, while she could have the girls. So my brothers went to Episcopalian schools and Confraternity of Christian Doctrine (CCD) classes on Saturdays, while I was sent off to Stone Ridge, one of the convent schools run by the nuns of the Sacred Heart order, from fourth through ninth grade. After that, my mother gave up on my Catholic education and let me go to an Episcopalian boarding school. She needed the house cleared of children, and she must have figured that by then I was deeply enough steeped in the religion.

When my father wrote home from England all those years ago that he'd fallen in love with the sixteen-year-old Catholic girl who would become his wife, his parents were surprised, not just by her age but by her religion. However, he'd had such a string of unsuitable love affairs that my New England Congregational grandparents were prepared to welcome anybody who could settle Stewart down. If she were what they called in whispered asides a "mackerel snatcher," they would adjust. So when my brother Joe was to be baptized in Avon in the summer of 1945, the only candidate they could find in town to stand in as godfather was John O'Neill, the Irish owner of the local automobile dealership. Everybody welcomed him at the baptismal font and at the reception afterward, but that was the last time any of us ever saw him.

To be a Roman Catholic in Washington social circles in the 1940s and 50s was odd. Kennedy hadn't come on the scene yet, and the patrician WASPs still held the reins of power. When my mother first got off the boat in 1945, she had an introduction to Lady Margaret Walker, who'd been a lady-in-waiting to Queen Elizabeth. Lady Margaret was married to John Walker, a curator at the National Gallery of Art, who later became my brother Ian's godfather. I think they were the only Catholics my parents knew in Washington. In March of 1948, when my mother was three months pregnant with me, the *Saturday Evening Post* featured her having tea with Lady Margaret in their elegant Georgetown house from the early 1800s. The two eldest Walker children are lying on the Persian rug reading a book, while my mother takes a teacup from Lady Margaret. Both women are dressed in black, which seems peculiar for an afternoon tea party, but the whole scene is obviously staged.

In her later years, I used to tease my mother that British Catholics were a breed unto themselves, the ones who had to prove that Henry VIII didn't exist. By that time, she'd developed a sense of humor about her religion, but that was not the case when we were growing up. We ate fish on Fridays, went to confession every Saturday, a three-hour vigil service on Good Friday, and mass on feast days as well as every Sunday. All the babies were baptized by the time they were a month old so they wouldn't end up in limbo—that halfway place between purgatory and hell, which has since been dropped as an official teaching of the church. While my brothers adopted my father's disaffected attitude, I took my cues from my mother. I wore a black-lace mantilla to church, dipped my hand in holy water on the way in and out, made the sign of the cross, closed my eyes in prayer and genuflected each time I crossed in front of the altar. If Mummy was a devout Catholic, then I'd try to be one too if that meant she might take more notice of me.

On Saturday afternoons, Mummy gathered us all up and herded us to confession through the side door of St. Ann's, the large gray stone edifice where, decades later, we held her funeral. She allowed us to disperse, although she kept a sharp eye on us from her own pew. Most of the time, I couldn't think of too many sins I'd committed, so often I made up sins on the spot, confessed them one week, and confessed to lying the next week.

The four confessionals were located in the corners of the church with the priest's name slid into the holder above the carved wooden door of his little room and we children roamed around choosing our line. Some of the priests were rumored to give lighter penances than others, but I was just trying to be sure I didn't end up in a line with Ian or Joe. Kneeling on one side of the priest with an eavesdropping brother waiting his turn on the other side would be the worst.

Mummy, who was usually finished way before the rest of us, had to bide her time, lighting candles for people's souls or reading the weekly newsletter. I was always attuned to her moods, and I often slipped into the pew next to her to say my penance, thinking my presence might still the impatient clock that seemed always to be ticking inside her.

⚬

Except for two times a year, Daddy didn't go to church. We'd find him relaxing over the newspaper as we were marched off to Sunday Mass. One morning, I stopped and asked him, "Why do we have to go to church and you don't?"

"Because you're being raised as Catholics and I'm an agnostic."

"What does that mean?"

"I don't believe or disbelieve in the existence of God."

"Maybe I'm an agnostic too."

"You're too young to decide. That's why I'm glad your mother is raising you in a specific religion. If you reject it, at least you'll know what you're rejecting."

My mother was honking the car horn.

"You're going to be late," he said, turning back to his paper.

"Did you go to church when you were my age?"

"I did. I was raised Episcopalian and had religion stuffed down my throat at boarding school. I know what I rejected. Off you go."

Mummy parked the car and led us up the center aisle to a front pew, where we sat in a solemn row, the physical evidence of her devotion to her faith. We took our cues from her, kneeling and standing when she did. She didn't tolerate whispering or fidgeting, and when it came time for Communion, she herded those of us who were old enough up the aisle to the rail to kneel and receive the wafer.

Unlike the boys, I didn't mind any of it. I liked imitating her movements, I loved the foreign sound of the Latin mass, the strange rhythmic chanting when even the tone-deaf priests had to worship the elevated host. After Mass, she drove us down Wisconsin Avenue to People's Drugstore where we were each allowed to choose two pieces of candy while she waited in the car. Maybe she considered this our reward for walking past our agnostic father every Sunday morning.

Twice a year, however, each Christmas and Easter, Daddy caved in and attended mass with us.

Mummy sat in the middle of the pew and my father took the aisle, which must have made him feel he could make his escape quickly. My brothers and I formed a row between them in easy reach should we need disciplining, although we rarely did. It was such an unusual experience to have our father in church with us that it drew our full attention. I could almost feel an electrical current running back and forth between my parents, as if my mother was worried that of all the bodies in the pew, my father was the one she'd have to discipline.

As the usher with the wicker offering basket drew nearer, my father took his wallet from his jacket pocket and pulled out a twenty and a five. He held them up, one in each hand, as if to study them, trying to decide how large his contribution would be. We snuck a glance at my mother, who was pretending not to notice. He waved them back and forth in the air as the basket got closer, until finally she couldn't stand it anymore. With an exasperated sigh, she reached across the four of us, snatched the twenty out of his fingers, and dropped it in the basket. My father grinned at us and pocketed the five. Sometimes if I looked quickly enough, I caught the shadow of a smile around my mother's lips. Twice a year, they put on this act.

There was a brief period in the seventh grade when I decided to become a nun. I set up an altar in my room with candles and a picture of Joan of Arc. (I'd taken Joan as my confirmation name.) My older two brothers had gone away to boarding school by then, but when they came home for Christmas vacation and discovered my new devotional self, they gave me such grief about it that I gave it up.

For my mother, the biggest problem that came with her religion was her fecundity; she simply couldn't stop having babies. Often, not long after my father came home from one of his extended overseas trips, she'd find herself pregnant again. In the end, she conceived twelve children: she birthed eight of us but lost two (a stillborn baby boy, and my sister who died at three months), and the other four were miscarriages (each one a boy). Ten boys and two girls. Her body was not her own. It belonged to the church.

~

My parents bought Polecat in the 1950s, during the Eisenhower period when Washington seemed dull and boring to my father. On a map, he drew a circle around Washington that represented an hour's driving distance from our house in the city and handed it to my mother. He told her that if she could find a place inside this circle that had at least 150 acres, a house, a pond for fishing, and didn't cost more than $15,000, he would buy it. I don't know how long it took her, but she did it. They bought 160 acres of land for one hundred dollars an acre with the wreck of a house thrown in for free. I think Daddy was surprised by her tenacity and what turned out to be her real estate smarts. (Years later, in the early 1970s, they sold the place for $150,000 and bought a baronial house near Harper's Ferry that used to belong to the Maryland branch of the Robert E. Lee family. And there was enough money left over to put in a swimming pool and a tennis court.)

Skunks in that part of Maryland were called polecats, so my parents christened the farm Polecat Park in honor of the family of skunks that had to be evicted from under the front porch when we moved in. For nineteen years, we spent most week-ends there and a month in the summer.

During the car trips out and back, the four of us children, stuffed into the rear seat of one or another of our second-hand station wagons, poked and badgered each other until my father called out "*Noli me tangere*"—his way of saying, "No touching, stop fighting, settle down"—in his sternest voice. It was the only time in the life of our family when we couldn't physically get away from each other. Driving along those back roads, we saw tumble-down houses where the yards had gone to weeds and cars were propped up on cinderblocks in various erratic positions, like children in a game of Statue. Daddy told us to look for the television antenna perched on the top of these shacks. "Always the television," he would marvel from the driv-er's seat. "Everything else can go to rack and ruin, but they always manage to afford a television." Lucky people, I thought. We didn't own a television until I was fourteen, and we only bought it then because my father had begun to appear on it from time to time.

At Polecat, we went to mass in a small, local church not far from the farm and by the time we got home, Daddy had nailed a paper plate to a tree at the end of the lawn for our rifle practice. There was no way I was going to miss out on target practice, so the photographs in the album show me, still in my smocked Sunday dress, leaning over the stock of the gun to aim at the bullseye. Mummy took those pictures, but soon afterward she would head into the kitchen to make lunch. All week long, as my father went about his business conducting interviews, he would invite people to Polecat, but by the time Sunday morning rolled around he could never remember who'd said yes. My mother knew that whatever she prepared had to accommodate as few as eight and as many as twenty.

Most of my parents' friends, like the Frank Wisners and the Philip Grahams, had large country estates on the fashionable Eastern shore and in Virginia with caretakers and staff. But these same people seemed just as happy to come to our run-down farm, where the only caretakers were a family who lived in the backwoods that my father nicknamed the Skonks. Mr. Skonk mowed our lawn and did various odd jobs and kept an eye on the place. The parents made brooms, and various dirty-looking children spilled out of the house into the mud-rutted front yard when we stopped by on a Sunday evening to pay the bill and check in with Mr. Skonk. I can't remember to this day what his real name was or if I ever knew it.

Interestingly, at Polecat, even though we had more space to roam free, Daddy spent time with us. Besides the target practice with the twenty-two-caliber rifle, he taught us how to shoot skeet with a twelve-gauge shotgun. We learned to gut and clean fish, and we knew we'd only be allowed to fish with him if we could kill the bass with a swift snap of its neck. As soon as we could see over the steering wheel, he taught us to drive up and down the bumpy dirt roads and let us take the car out by ourselves as long as we stayed on the property. (My teenage friends and I spent hours bouncing through the muddy holes and smoking our forbidden cigarettes. Years later, my mother told me there was so much smoke floating out our open windows that the car looked like a cloud drifting along the horizon at the edge of the field.) On the way home on Sunday nights, we always stopped at the diner where Daddy could get a beer with his meal, and to keep us quiet, he'd hand out quarters so each of us could pick three songs on the jukebox. Our supper never lasted as long as the songs, so we jostled to be the first one to choose. Last person in line might as well pocket the quarter.

My favorite photograph from that time shows my father in his customary weekend outfit, which consisted of a pair of stained khaki shorts and one of his white business shirts with the sleeves rolled up his arms. He is sitting on the steps of the front porch, his elbows resting on his knees and his hands dangling casually between his legs. His eyes are locked on some distant object, and his thoughts too are far away. I look to be about six, and since I'm wearing a dress, I know I must have just returned from mass. I have maneuvered my way inside the circle formed by his arms, and with my head to the side and a gleeful grin on my face, I am busy mussing up his black hair. My mother, always the photographer, takes three shots right in a row. His stance never changes. He does not move or acknowledge me as I cavort around inside the magic space but waits patiently for me to be done with my fooling without letting it distract him from his thoughts. Even when he was there physically, he was often somewhere else in his mind. It's a writer's curse. Because I have it too, I was more forgiving of my father's dreamy absences than my mother's.

In the albums from those years, my mother looks sadly absent. Sitting on the porch or in a chair by the pond, she stares into the distance, chewing on the edge of her thumb. She's wearing one of Daddy's shirts, almost always a string of pearls, and her favorite deep red lipstick, which means that guests are expected and soon she'll have to go back to the kitchen. In one photo, a book is open on her lap and the barrel of a rifle is poking through the slats in the chair next to hers where Daddy's tackle box rests on the wide arm. I can imagine that the oldest of her four children are splashing about in the pond or she's watching our rifle practice from the porch. But she's not really present, always staring, always thinking about something else or traveling back to the life she had before this one or the one she might have had if she'd made a different decision at the age of eighteen.

Tish reading by the Pond at Polecat

Then the guests would arrive, tumbling out of their cars with a great slamming of doors and "Did you bring a towel for me?" and "God, Stew, you're going to have to do something with that bloody road," and "let's swim first." With drinks and cigarettes in hand, the men and women trailed down the slope talking loudly to each other about politics or the latest scandal in the government or teasing my father about the state of his fly rods or his swimming trunks or the pond.

A typical Sunday might include Tom and Joan Braden with some of their eight children, Bob Joyce with his thick, fierce eyebrows, sly smile and gravelly voice, and his wife Jane, the only woman of their age who dared to wear a tiny bikini, Bill

Walton, the painter and Kennedy intimate who loved to play bridge, and Mary and Bill Bundy, an analyst for the CIA and brother of the more famous Mac. My uncle Joe came if he hadn't gotten a better invitation to some chic place on the Eastern shore. The Bissells and Rowly Evans, the *Herald Tribune* reporter, and his wife, Kay, were regulars, but every Sunday, the list shifted.

As soon as my mother greeted the new arrivals, she'd retreat to the primitive kitchen, a seedy room down three sloping steps from the dining room, where all the metal drawers were rusted at the corners and stuck in their tracks. The appliances were as old as the house, and the green and black checked linoleum had small volcanic lumps and bumps across its surface, as if the rot beneath the boards was pushing upwards.

The pond was spring fed, an oval-shaped body of water at the bottom of a long hill. My father had dammed it up at one end and stocked it with bass, but every summer, as the water heated up, the green algae that covered the surface would get thicker and smellier. On Sunday mornings, while we were at mass and before the guests arrived, he rowed himself around the pond in a small dinghy, dragging one of his black silk socks packed with copper sulfate, a green crystallized chemical, which seeped out through the thin material and broke down the blue-green scum.

He built a homemade raft from a green wooden trellis ripped off the side of the porch. This was hammered on to a string of canvas-covered rings, the kind that are tossed off ships to drowning people. We all learned to take care crossing this makeshift raft to the ladder, because if somebody was coming the other way, it would tip back and forth in a wild rocking motion. More than one guest had fallen off into the deep, oozy mud near the shore, and when the boys were on the raft, they tipped it on purpose, trying to throw each other off.

One day before I knew how to swim, I stood on the grassy shore and watched as the boys and their friends lined up so they could sprint along the rickety raft and hurl themselves into the water shouting "Geronimo" and splashing the ladies while pretending not to. With my mother in the kitchen, Daddy, for once, tried to be the disciplinarian.

"Stop it, all of you," he roared from the far side of the pond. He never cared much for swimming. With his fly rod held high above the surface, he sank his bottom into one of the inner tubes from tires that we used as floats and kicked his way across to the shade under the evergreens, as far from the noise of the swimmers as he could get. Then he cast his line into the quiet spot where the largest of the stocked bass congregated in the summer.

"Stew," Mrs. Evans called after another round of splashing. "They're really impossible."

"All right. I'm coming," he called as he reeled in the fly, settled the rod across his knees and paddled back to restore order.

Watching all this, I formed the idea that I didn't need an inner tube anymore. After all, swimming took nothing more than a little courage and a daring leap. So, in the middle of the melee, when nobody was paying attention, I walked to the ladder, stared down into the murky water, took a deep breath and jumped. I shot down like a rocket and the water rushed up my nose. Even though I pushed my arms around in circles the way I'd seen the swimmers do on the surface, nothing happened. I did not move in any direction. My feet sank into the cold ooze at the bottom of the pond. I was drowning right in the middle of a noisy swimming party.

Up above, someone must have noticed.

Faintly, through the murky water, I heard my name called once, and then again. A hand brushed against me. Strong fingers closed around my upper arm and my father pulled me up with one swift movement, the way you yank a plug out of a drain. Without a word, he deposited me like a package on the raft where the Sunday guests took over. Somebody slapped me on the back until I threw up a mouthful of pond water. One lady wrapped me in a towel, walked me across the raft and handed me over to another on the shore, who hugged me against her wet belly, swathed in a flowered, skirted suit. I kept my eyes closed the whole time because I didn't want to look at the boys.

Later, when there were no grown-ups around to hush them, my brothers hooted with laughter at their hopeless sister, who thought the only thing you needed to know about swimming was how to get into the water.

I never told my mother that I might have drowned while she was in the kitchen preparing lunch. Actually, this book could be titled, *The Things I Never Told My Mother*. They would include the time Joe bugged my bedroom, or the time Rich Bissell tried to fool with me when he chased me to the far side of the pond, or the man at Ellen's Gift Shop who twice slid his hands inside my underpants while I was picking out china horses for my collection.

When she did notice that something might be "off," it was usually afterward.

"Do you want to stop at Ellen's Gift Shop on the way back?" she asked one day when she was driving me to the dentist.

"No, thanks," I said.

"You don't collect china horses anymore?"

"Nope." She hadn't noticed that they were gone, packed into two shoeboxes in the top of my closet.

"Why not?"

I shrugged. "I'm too old for that," I said which wasn't true, but she didn't press.

She never knew about the time, not long after the second violation by the man in the gift shop, when I took the boxes down to the lower driveway and smashed each horse with a flat rock I found nearby. When it was all done and there was nothing left but sparkly dust, I trudged back up the hill, threw the shoeboxes in the trash, and put myself to bed. By the time the maid called me for dinner, my parents had already gone out. I told her I had a stomachache and she let me be.

As the only daughter, I made it my job to be the easy child, the one who never made trouble or reported violations or demanded attention, the one who figured she could take care of herself, though deep down, she knew she wasn't very good at it.

For me, Polecat started and ended with snakes. We got rid of the polecats living under the front porch, but we never got rid of the black snakes. My father used to remind us that they ate the rats and mice, but I didn't like the look of them. They lay in the sun on the tops of rocks near the pond and they slunk around in the dark places under the barn. If one slithered by too close to the house, my mother insisted my father get rid of it and he'd shoot it with the twenty-two-caliber rifle. Afterward, one of us kids would be allowed to use the rifle, empty of ammunition, to scoop up the dead body and carry it to the dump. That was a job I loved, especially the moment when, with the others watching, I twisted the rifle over my shoulder and hurled that black snake, still jerking in his death throes, high in the air until finally it dropped into a distant mound of trash on the far side of the dump.

One summer in my early teens, I found a black snake curled in the toilet bowl of the second-floor bathroom. With my shorts around my knees, I ran out of the bathroom screaming for my father, but by the time he got upstairs with the gun, the snake had slithered away down the wall, leaving a wet trail that ended in the metal grill of the ancient radiator.

That was it for me. I roamed the house all night watching for snakes. I saw them crawling up the faded chintz curtains, I saw them wound in and out of the curly brass arms of the dining room chandelier, I imagined a tangled pile of them in every toilet. How could my family continue to sleep peacefully in their beds when the house was infested with reptiles? At three in the morning, I forced myself to climb the stairs to my parent's room and knock on their door. This showed how scared I must have been, because even at Polecat, their bedroom was strictly off limits. I'd tried as hard as I could to wait out the night, but this time I couldn't make it. I was too scared. I knocked again. Slowly the door opened, and my mother came out in her filmy nightgown. When I told her that the snakes were everywhere in the house, she led me back to my bed, across the room from my younger brother, and tucked me in, telling me that I was imagining things. I pretended to fall asleep so that she didn't have to stay up any longer, but the moment she went back to her room, I sat up so I could take up watch again. My bed shared a wall with the bathroom where now I was sure I could hear the snake sliding up through the radiator coils.

After that, I begged weekend invitations from classmates or convinced my parents I was old enough to stay alone in town, so I'd never have to go back to Polecat. When my parents finally decided to sell the house it was not because of the snakes but because the encroaching suburbs of Washington drove them farther out into the country.

BODIES

1958–1960

Soon after Joe started boarding school, my mother got pregnant again, this time with my fourth brother, Nick. She'd just managed to move one of us out of the house and already another was on the way. Through most of that pregnancy, she drank heavily. Ian, who got home from school first, would wait for me at the kitchen door to give me the report on her mood. If her car was in the driveway, I might get the thumbs-up sign which meant she was around and acting "normal." Thumbs-down meant she was locked in her bedroom and if she came out, we knew to scatter and hide.

With Joe gone from our daily lives, Ian and I had tried to keep up our basement life, but it felt strangely lonely down there. We were adrift without our commander and looked for other places in the house to hide. One of our favorites was Jessie's room on the third floor. Of the succession of maids who took care of us when we were growing up, Jessie's is the only name I remember, perhaps because it was so musical. Jessie May Jefferson Tucker.

Both my parents grew up with caregiving women who stayed in their households for their entire childhoods and beyond. My father and his siblings had Aggie who was such a central figure in their lives that all three boys wrote letters to her when they were away at war. At the end of my father's letter announcing to his parents that he had proposed to my mother, he added a postscript: *Tell Aggie I'll always love her, but it looks finally as though I'll have to divorce her.* My mother never had a governess or nanny who played such a central part in her life, but she remembers with great affection Josefa, a nurse to her grandmother who is buried with her grandparents in their above-ground vault in Gibraltar.

When it came to our upbringing, however, it seemed that my mother, who did all the hiring, couldn't get good help. Young and inexperienced when she arrived in this country, she wanted to bring in Spanish-speaking women like the ones she'd had as a child in Gibraltar, but my father steadfastly refused because he didn't speak the language. It wasn't until my youngest brother was born that she defied Daddy and sponsored Olga and her daughter Nora from El Salvador who moved into the third floor with Nora's son, Jose Mario. So, my two youngest brothers, Andrew and Nick, had a consistent presence in the house to care for them all the times when my parents were absent. We older four kids only had that sense of safety during the summers we spent in Avon with our grandmother and our times there remain our happiest childhood memories. Aggie, with her piercing blue eyes, white hair, and faint Scottish burr and Emma Wenz, the cook, whose kitchen smelled of chocolate chip cookies and apple pie, welcomed us every year for weeks at a time. In the afternoons, cousins who lived nearby joined us for tea with Grandmother on the sun porch where we sat on yellow crinkly plastic cushions and answered her piercing questions. But it was in the kitchen and the back dining room reserved for us children where we felt most comfortable.

Recently, when I asked my younger brother Stewart what he remembers about the time he blew up his hand by lighting a line of gunpowder on his bedroom windowsill, he told me that it happened in October of 1963 when Daddy was reporting from Moscow, and Mummy was visiting her mother in Gibraltar. Daddy's secretary, an eccentric red-haired woman named Miss Puff, was staying in the house to supervise whichever maid was currently on the job so she was the first to respond to the sound of the explosion and Stewart's screams. She ordered the maid to bundle up his hand in towels, tossed Stewart into her VW bug, and drove him to the hospital to get stitches. The name of the maid, I ask. He doesn't remember. That's the way it always is with us oldest four. We only refer to them as the maids. Except for one.

I don't remember when Jessie Mae Jefferson Tucker came to us or how long she lasted. I do remember that she brought her own television, a luxury we didn't have.

The third floor was considered off-limits to us children unless we were expressly invited. After all, the maids needed their retreat from the chaos and downstairs demands, and they deserved their privacy. The accommodations were hardly luxurious. If my mother had managed to employ two people at a time, they each took a bedroom; both rooms were tucked up under the eaves across the landing from one another. If not, the single maid used the second bedroom as a sitting room. Besides the three storage areas, which were really no more than crawl spaces, and the landing at the top of the stairs, there was a disreputable bathroom with barely enough space for a shower stall, a minuscule sink, and a toilet.

Jessie was there on her own, but she used the smaller of the two bedrooms. Luckily, she was short, because nobody over five foot four could stand up straight where the sloping roof cut into the eastern wall. The General Electric table model TV sat on the bureau so that she could watch it at night from her bed. It didn't have an antenna, but because she lived right under the roof the reception wasn't bad. The screen measured about sixteen inches from one corner to the other, so you had to sit pretty close to pick up the nuances of the show—which, in my case, was always lady wrestling. The only other item on the bureau that sticks in my mind was a squat blue bottle of pomade that Jessie used to slick down her hair every morning.

Ian sometimes watched with me, but unbeknownst to him, Jessie and I made a secret deal just between us. On the nights my parents went out for dinner, she liked to pack up the remains of the fried chicken she'd made for us in a paper bag and go out herself. Who knows where? I never asked. But as long as I didn't tell my parents that she'd left us alone, she let me sneak upstairs to her room afternoons after school to watch lady wrestling.

The muscled women, dressed in bathing suits or tight

two-pieces, grunted and sweated and grimaced at one another and slammed their opponents' bodies to the ground. One would catch the other's head between the ropes or between her legs. They had nicknames like Lipstick and Dynamite. They flipped bodies, grabbed hair, dropped to their knees on the other's chest. Watching it now, I can see that it was mostly choreographed. The more violent the move, the more the crowd egged them on, screaming for blood. I was fascinated and horrified both, but time and again, the third floor called to me. With Joe away at school and Ian soon to follow, our tightly formed pack was breaking up but even if the boys had stayed home, I would have been pushed out. Those heaving women exposing their sweaty bodies couldn't have been more different than the women I saw around me: nuns swathed in black from head to toe, the maids in their pastel uniforms, and my mother, always appropriately covered and often large with child. Under my rag-tag hand-me-downs, I could feel my body changing. I was ready to try on different female roles, but while the power of the lady wrestlers stirred me, I also found it too foreign and frightening. Mothering seemed safer, so when Jessie stole out after my parents left for dinner, I appointed myself the second-floor monitor.

This arrangement made me even more vigilant than before as I lay awake listening to the house noises. Stewart's bedroom was next to mine, so when he woke up with a nightmare on one of Jessie's "nights out," I settled him down. Joe was at Groton, and Ian slept at the other end of the hallway away from the foot traffic. Sometimes when I heard a strange noise downstairs and was feeling particularly brave, I'd tiptoe down to investigate. Other times, I'd just put my head under the pillow and tell myself it was the furnace or a squirrel on the roof. I kept up my part of the bargain, and on the nights she was gone, I stayed awake until I heard the car drive in and my parents walking up the stairs. They assumed all along that Jessie was asleep in the attic, and I never heard her come home.

Once Jessie left, there were others. I do remember one, a

thin, sad drunk named Esther, who finally got out of hand. My mother had to bribe a taxi driver to wrestle her down from the third floor as she alternated between protestations of innocence and apologies.

"So sorry, ma'am. So sorry. Promise I won't do it again."

My mother was unmoved. The taxi driver managed to lock Esther in his cab while he went back upstairs to get her belongings.

☙

My mother was never a fashionable dresser. When she was growing up in Gibraltar, her mother and the dressmaker chose all her clothes. During the war in England, when they couldn't get their hands on extra material, she made do with one or two outfits for work and a Sunday dress for church. For her wedding, she'd had her tennis dress, the only white outfit in her closet, altered for the ceremony. She was someone who made do and was proud of it.

But when she came to America, my uncle Joe decided that "making do" wasn't good enough. As he wrote to a friend, *Tish looked ethereal and lovely; but she seemed to have done her hair by butting a hedge-fence; and her clothes appeared to have been thrown at her, more or less at random, by a rather tasteless friend standing at a considerable distance.* As he felt that Stew and Tish were *letting down the partnership*, he took over, as he was prone to do. He designed my mother's clothes, ordered dresses from his Hong Kong tailor, and took her shopping at Dorcas Hardin, the chic Georgetown dress shop that she wouldn't have dared enter on her own.

So, it's not surprising that she had no idea how to dress an American girl. My mother seemed to find all her children mystifying, but me most of all, perhaps because I came after the two boys or because she'd never had a sister or because she and her mother weren't close.

One day, on the way to school in carpool, I asked her if I could have a bra.

Without thinking, she said, "But whatever for, dear?"

She was right, of course. I didn't even have the breasts for a training bra, but sitting in the front seat next to her, I shrank away into silence and prayed she wouldn't bring it up again. She didn't.

In the sixth grade, when I was the last girl in dancing school still wearing black patent leather shoes and little white socks, I screwed up my courage and asked her if I could please have stockings.

She looked as if she found this request peculiar.

"Really? What color?"

What color? Aren't all stockings the same color? The question threw me so far off that my mind went completely blank. She was waiting for an answer. Whenever my mother had to wait on one of us, I could sense a tapping foot, a ticking clock. Her patience was running out.

"Black," I blurted out, the first thing that came to mind.

She frowned, and then shrugged. "Black? Are you sure?"

No, of course I didn't want black stockings. What a ridiculous idea. *Mummy, forget that,* I wanted to say. *Why did you ask me for a color? Stockings don't have a color. They look like your legs.* But the conversation was over and I couldn't think of a way to rewind the tape. The next day, I found a pair of black tights on my bed. Thick black tights. The kind they probably wore in England when she went to the Catholic boarding school with its drafty rooms and no central heat.

What mother would send her twelve-year-old daughter to dancing school in a blue, smocked, short-sleeved dress with a white collar ordered by her grandmother from Harrods in London and black wool tights?

Mine.

Since Ian and I were only thirteen months apart, we were enrolled in the same class at Miss Shippen's dancing school. As we headed out the door to get into the car where my mother was waiting, my father, settled in his comfortable easy chair in the living room, put down his paper for a moment to look at me.

"Good heavens," he remarked. "Next time I see you, you'll be reading *Mein Kampf.*"

I had no idea what he was talking about, but I was worried. Instead of fading into the crowd of girls lined up on one side of the room or primping in the bathroom, I was going to stand out like a sore thumb. I should have stuck with the little white socks.

It seemed the two hours would never end. Even Miss Shippen, who usually sat like Queen Victoria in stern, lumpish silence on her throne at one end of the room, gasped as I passed by. Nobody actually pointed, but I could feel the eyes burning into my back and I could hear the muffled whispers and giggles. Later, Ian told me that he took pity on me and bribed one boy to dance with me. (He was sympathetic because in those days nobody else was named Ian, so he was often listed as Jan Alsop at the top of the girls' column in the attendance book.) His classmate Al Gore, of all people, steered me woodenly around the room in the one obligatory dance they'd agreed to and hurriedly returned to the boys' side to collect his dollar.

I went back to the white socks until I could save enough allowance to buy my own stockings at Murphy's Five and Dime on Wisconsin Avenue. If my mother noticed, she didn't mention it.

I got my period much later than other girls in my class. One fall during one of Granny's annual visits, I casually repeated something I'd heard in the school locker room about having bad cramps. My grandmother shot my mother a knowing look and they went into a huddle upstairs. Next thing I knew, my mother called me into her bedroom and handed me a box of Kotex, a belt, and a book entitled *Know Your Body*.

"You might need these," she said, with Granny nodding sagely in the background.

She didn't elaborate and I didn't ask questions. That was my way. If I didn't understand something, I'd go away and try to figure it out rather than admit I was out of the loop. "You might need these," constituted my mother's entire discussion with me on the subject of sex.

The book was useless. I sold it to Ian for a dollar. After considering the rest of the equipment for a while, I decided the soft pads were meant to soothe my stomachache. So that evening, I went down to dinner in a tight sweater with a pad stretched across my belly, secured at either side of my waist by the belt. If my mother and grandmother noticed the strange long lump, they didn't say a word.

After dinner, I threw the unsoiled Kotex in my trash can and thought no more about it until the next day, when the maid of the moment came up to my room and presented me with a small paper bag. In a whisper, she said, "Elizabeth, there are boys in the house." She stopped and looked at me with a long, knowing look. Duh, I thought. Then she went on. "Whenever you are at that time of the month, you just let me know, and I'll make sure you have one of these in your wastepaper basket to discard the pads."

Pathetic as it is to admit all these years later, I literally had no idea what any of these women were talking about. Was the wastepaper basket code for something else? Why was it necessary to hide the pads in a paper bag? Finally, I gave up and called my best friend, Vicky. I hated admitting I didn't know something, but I was desperate to understand all these coded messages. She invited me over to spend the night and all was made clear. Her mother had explained sex to her older sister, who immediately passed it all on to Vicky, and she to me.

Role Models

1959–1960

I looked for other mothers. My grandmother helped during the summer visits to the Connecticut farm or her house on Long Island Sound, but still we saw her mainly at teatime, when she'd ask about the story I was writing or who I'd challenged that week on the club tennis ladder. I loved her and always felt completely safe in Avon and on the shore, but I spent most of my time in the kitchen because, after Aggie died, Emma, the cook, provided food and if not hugs, at least consistent and loving attention.

Alice Roosevelt Longworth—nicknamed "Mrs. L."—was another constant presence in my life. In the years between the departures of Joe and Ian, for boarding school and my own, I had tea with her once a week.

Most days, I traveled to and from school in a carpool, but on Thursday afternoons I got a ride home in Mrs. L.'s black Cadillac, which pulled into the circular driveway by the front door of Stone Ridge, my Catholic day school. She was the only person allowed to pick up at the front, which meant she could avoid the chaotic dismissal at the lower entrance. I loved Thursdays. Mrs. L.—or Cousin Alice, as my father called her—was my grandmother's first cousin and Theodore Roosevelt's daughter. She lived in a four-story stone house near Dupont Circle with her granddaughter, Joanna, who also went to Stone Ridge.

Once Turner, Mrs. L.'s chauffeur, had opened the back door for me and Joanna, he would return to the driver's seat. My clearest memory of Turner is of his grizzled hair and the black folds of his neck between the dark cap and the white collar of his uniform. We stopped first to drop Joanna at a farm near the school where she rode Arabian horses a couple of days a week. Then I had Mrs. L. all to myself.

Alice Roosevelt Longworth, known as Mrs. L......

She sat in the back next to me in full lotus position on what seemed to me plush velvet upholstery, because I was used to the grubby rear seat of my mother's secondhand, overused station wagon. Often elegantly costumed in a silk luncheon dress, she always wore a wide-brimmed black straw hat perched above a cloud of pale-yellow hair, secured in a twist in the back. When wisps drifted down around her thin face, she swept them out of the way with an impatient wave of her hand. She had flashing blue eyes, pale porcelain skin, delicate bones and a wicked, mischievous look that settled on her face when she put the index finger of her right hand up to her lips and contemplated you.

Sometimes she'd start reciting bits of the *Rubaiyat of Omar Khayyam* or launch into a famous first line of poetry like, "In Xanadu, did Kubla Khan, a stately pleasure dome decree." She was famous for her photographic memory, but she saved her poetry recitations for me alone because Joanna accused her of showing off. "Grammy," she'd warn, and roll her eyes. Once we'd dropped Joanna at her riding lesson, I played the eager audience, happy to be wrapped in that cocoon with Mrs. L. and Turner as he wove his way into Washington.

Mrs. L. didn't have a license, but she never hesitated to comment on Turner's driving, which was erratic to say the least. We used to say that Turner drove by ear. There'd be a little jolt on one side of the car, and Mrs. L. would call out, "Turner, I think you hit something back there."

And Turner would nod his head calmly. "Yes, ma'am, I believe I did."

And on we'd go without another mention of the unfortunate incident. Turner was unflappable, a solid dark presence in the front seat as he maneuvered the old car through the streets of Washington, one eye on the road and the other on the rearview mirror. Every so often he would chuckle to himself over something Mrs. L or I said to each other. To the great irritation of all around us, he drove very slowly and with a gentle weaving motion which made it impossible to pass him. Cars were always honking at us, and many times, a driver would be forced into some wildly irresponsible maneuver simply to get away from our slow and unpredictable progress. The other car would shoot past us in the wrong lane, and I have fleeting memories of enraged expressions and crazed poundings of palms against horns. Turner acted as if these people didn't exist. They seemed to make no impression at all on his attention or his placid exterior.

Our destination was Mrs. L.'s living room on the second floor of her Dupont Circle house. Once we were ensconced on her sofa with the famous pillow that read, "If you can't say something good about someone sit right here by me," Janey the maid brought in the old-fashioned silver tea service. My grandmother had one of these too, and I loved the ceremony of it. Real tea leaves (usually a smoky Chinese brand like Lapsang souchong) floated inside the silver teapot which sat on its own little stand above a flickering blue flame. When it had steeped long enough, Mrs. L. or Janey, taking care to touch only the wooden section of the handle, tilted the spout forward so that the boiling dark liquid flowed through a silver strainer into the delicate china cup. The tray held a plate with lemon slices and a bowl of sugar cubes, each with its own silver tongs, two linen napkins and a salver of paper-thin cookies. I added three sugar cubes to my tea with no comment at all from Mrs. L. We sat back and stirred with our spoons until, sooner or later, she'd start to ask me questions. They weren't the usual adult queries about "How was school?" and "What book are you reading?" Oh no. Like so many other people in Washington, what Mrs. L wanted was information, and she knew I was a reliable source. She'd ask who'd come to our house for dinner that week, or who my father had interviewed in our living room, and had Mrs. Braden been over to see my mother, and what in God's name was she wearing this week, and so on. All my spying came in handy as I offered up what tidbits I could, the dues I paid for the ride in the Cadillac and the cups of real tea and most importantly, the treat of her full and undivided attention. When Turner drove back out to the horse farm to pick up Joanna, he'd drop me off at the end of our driveway in time for supper at home.

Mrs. L. and I avoided subjects like my mother's mood or my father's travels, although she certainly was aware of the tensions in our house. She pretended that all was fine and I joined her in that fiction. My mother had a real affection for Mrs. L. Not long after Joanna's parents died, Mummy suggested that Joanna could live with us during the week, go to school with me, and move to her grandmother's on weekends. She thought it would be easier for Joanna to live with a family, but Mrs. L. said no. She was grateful to Mummy for the offer, but she would be raising Joanna herself. They were an odd couple, the famous grandmother and her smart, prickly granddaughter, but in the end, they became the best of friends. When my younger brother Nick was born, Mummy chose thirteen-year-old Joanna to be his godmother.

Recently I received a note from a professor in England who had unearthed several interviews with Mrs. L. that had never been transcribed. He thought I might be especially interested in the two minutes she spent describing me at the age of six. As my mother told Mrs. L., I was a very shy child, but apparently with no provocation, I liked to imitate Mrs. L.'s voice. And she loved it.

She had an upper class, faux English accent that even she knew sounded odd in twentieth-century America. "I speak in a way that is absurd and I know it. And there are a handful of words like 'uh-uh-ah' that amuse the child. I've never heard anything as funny as she was. I said, 'You're a minx! You're a baggage.' And up to now, I thought she was a dear little quiet prim child who sat one foot slightly advanced, the other slightly behind that foot with a little ribbon in your hair, your little hands folded in your lap. And you're a wicked child. Just the way I had said to her, 'I thought you were a prim little child,' and she said, 'I thought you were a prim little child,' right after me. We became the kind of friends that never have been; we laughed until we cried and then I got her to do more imitations of me."

I have no memory of this encounter, but no wonder we remained such good friends. To this day, I'm delighted to know that I was praised as a wicked child by the original wicked child.

As President Roosevelt once said of his daughter, Alice, "I can be President of the United States, or I can control Alice. I cannot possibly do both."

Joan Braden adopted me for a while, folded me into the pack of children that her husband, Tom, would write about in his book, *Eight is Enough*. She did shop at Dorcas Hardin all by herself, and always wore the latest style, whether—as the Washington matrons would sniff—it suited her or not. She was bright, bouncy, thin, chic, and flirtatious, everything my mother was not. My memories of her come back as brief snapshots: the time she bought me a dirndl dress in Aspen, Colorado, so I could be photographed with her five girls, all in the same outfits. Once, she and her daughter Mary and I arrived early at Polecat and sat on the porch watching the drizzle and waiting for my parents who had the key. While Mary and I sank our bottoms into the deep *V* of the Adirondack chairs, Mrs. Braden belted out, "Singing in the Rain," all the while imitating Gene Kelly, tip tapping across the cement porch. One time she took me and Mary to the 1964 World's Fair in New York, where we were photographed by a roving cameraman who was hoping we'd order a copy of the picture. Mary and I look shy and uncomfortable while Mrs. Braden's smile is so wide and white that her eyes almost disappear into her suntanned California wrinkles. She approached the world assuming it was her oyster, and next to her, other women often felt somber and dowdy. I know my mother did. Since my father had met Tom Braden during the war, when they both volunteered for the Kings Royal Rifle Corps, my mother allowed us to become entangled with the Bradens for the sake of that friendship. But she rarely relaxed when Joan was around.

When I wasn't watching the lady wrestlers or attaching myself to other peoples' mothers, I tried on other roles. With the boys gone, I made friends at my convent school and went on silent weekend retreats where the priest seemed obsessed with cautioning us against sex and detailing for us when a boy's hand on our thigh turned from a venial to a mortal sin. My friends and I laughed about it afterward, and they were always sneaking around the grounds of the school during those weekends, trying to get far enough away from the nuns so they could break the vow of silence. I never admitted how much I liked the quiet, how safe I felt with just my own thoughts unlike on normal days when I was on edge, trying to fit in.

One day, I stapled my palms in imitation of Christ's stigmata. It hurt like crazy, but I was eager to make an impression on Mother Mahaney, my favorite nun. She was the tall, skinny one who rolled her black habit up to her knees while coaching the basketball team. When I showed her my bleeding palms, she sent me to the infirmary with the admonition that, "God does not like showoffs."

Soon after Nick was born in July of 1959, my father left on a two-month, three-thousand-mile reporting trip through Eastern Europe. I proved efficient with the baby, and I was happy to hold and feed him, partially because I enjoyed it, but also because I knew my mother was desperate to get away from the crying demands of a newborn. I could make her life easier. Maybe I could even keep her from locking herself away in the bedroom. It didn't work, but I kept trying.

I got my real chance to play mother the following June, when Nick was eleven months old and my mother went away with Mrs. Bissell to a rest place called Billy Budd's. The baby was fussy at night, and with the maids sleeping on the third floor, I was often the one who got to his crib first. I loved it when he put out his arms for me. Mummy came home after a month, dressed in an oversized Billy Budd sweatshirt, and as I learned later from family correspondence, "on the wagon." Her hair was long and lank, and she looked paler and more fragile than before. Although she didn't physically disappear as often into her secret lair in the bedroom, she was more obviously emotionally absent. Her manner was subdued, her voice flat, almost subservient, as if she'd been hypnotized or brainwashed into submission.

Her first night home, she and Daddy went to Uncle Joe's for dinner. Uncle Joe had promised his sister-in-law that no one at all would be there her first night. He didn't bother to mention that he'd invited JFK to drop in that afternoon for a chat, as he assumed the candidate would be gone long before my parents were due for their quiet family meal. But Kennedy guzzled one cup of tea after another, all the while talking about his prospects and the upcoming convention in Los Angeles. It must have been disconcerting for my mother to find the leading Democratic candidate sitting on Uncle Joe's sofa when it was supposed to be just family. Uncle Joe reported that she looked very thin, and that being on the wagon had reduced her to the limp, shy, silent teenager Daddy had brought home from England fifteen years before. But a few nights later, she seemed to have recovered her tongue and her energy. Everybody breathed a sigh of relief, assuming that Mummy's "very grave problem" had been solved.

A few days after that, Ian and I flew with Daddy and Uncle

Joe to California. Uncle Joe and Phil Graham, the publisher
of the *Washington Post*, had just recommended that Kennedy
choose Lyndon Johnson as a running mate, so the grown-ups
were all abuzz. Uncle Joe described it in a letter from Washington to his future wife, Susan Mary Patten, in Paris: *Tish, Stew, and*
four children are coming to lunch in an hour, before Stew, two children, and
I fly to California, the two elders for the Democratic convention, and the
children for one of the various rest homes, provided free by friends, where
Stew deposits his young for the summer. The rest home that summer
for Ian and myself was the Braden's house in Oceanside, where
we were folded into their pack of then six children. Joe went
to camp, Mummy stayed home with the younger two, and in
August, after the convention, we were all to meet in Aspen,
Colorado, for a big Braden-Alsop family vacation.

Joan Braden hired keepers for her children much the way my
mother did. Off the parents went to the convention, leaving
us in the care of a woman named Maria and her common-law
husband, Jimmy. Maria and Jimmy fought all the time, and
whenever he ventured into the kitchen, she laid a large butcher
knife out on the counter to give him fair warning that he'd better watch out. Jimmy was a tall, skinny African American man
with long pomaded hair combed straight back off his forehead.
He lurked around the house and sometimes popped up when
you were least expecting him. David and Mary, the oldest Braden children, and Ian and I, spent most of our days wandering
Cassidy Street Beach, watching the surfers. The younger Braden
girls, Joanie, Susan, Nancy, and Elizabeth, all milled around Maria, crawling in and out of her lap and hanging on to her legs
while she stood at the stove.

The other visitor that summer was an eighteen-year-old
Harvard freshman named Steve Schlesinger whose father, Arthur, was a Kennedy advisor. Steve had the use of one of the
Braden cars and a job at the Oceanside newspaper *Blade Tribune*,
which Tom Braden owned at the time. We didn't see much of
Steve—as he himself admitted later, he spent most of his time
cruising in the car, trying unsuccessfully to pick up girls. When

the adults returned from the convention, we were told that all eight of us children were to be driven to Aspen, Colorado, in two cars: Jimmy and Maria in one, and Steve driving the other. Nobody seemed to worry that Steve had just gotten his license and was expected to drive over a thousand miles with several young children in his car.

We older four piled in with Steve while the younger girls rode with Jimmy and Maria. Jimmy made it clear to Steve that he was to follow orders for the entire trip. He would drive directly behind Jimmy, he would gas up when Jimmy did, pull over when Jimmy signaled, and so on.

This system lasted half a day. Steve hated it, and we were all scared of Jimmy who could be very menacing. Once, when he thought Steve hadn't followed closely enough, he waved us over, walked back to the car and stuck his head right in the driver's side when Steve reluctantly rolled down the window.

"Don't leave a car between us, you understand," he barked. "You stay right behind me."

Steve shrugged, Jimmy withdrew, and we started up again.

But the next time Jimmy pulled over to gas up, Steve muttered, "I'm not doing this anymore."

"What do you mean?" I asked nervously.

"We're going to get to Aspen on our own. Hold on."

He waited until the attendant had begun to gas up Jimmy's car, then pulled around and took off. I don't remember squealing tires, but there might have been. We four kids ducked down in the back as if we were in the getaway car and the police were chasing us, all guns blazing. It felt that way. The last time we saw Jimmy, he was standing shouting at us with his fist pumping the air.

"Will my sisters be okay?" Mary asked, lifting her head from the musty seat back.

"Maria will take care of them," Steve said. "She'll make Jimmy behave." I thought of the knife and wondered if Maria had brought it along.

We drove and drove. Steve was too scared to stop in case

Jimmy caught up with us. We took turns sitting in the front seat and every so often, when he felt himself dozing off, he'd remind one of us to throw water in his face to help him stay awake.

To Steve's amazement, we got to Aspen first, but what was even more surprising when I think back on it, is how casually we were welcomed. Nobody asked why we hadn't stuck with Jimmy and Maria or where the four younger girls were. Mrs. Braden directed Steve to leave us four at the rented house in town, until the other car arrived. This was the usual arrangement on these family vacations. The adults stayed in cabins up in the mountains on the banks of the Roaring Fork River while the children slept downtown in big modern houses with bunk beds, pine-paneled walls and not much furniture. Packs of us roamed the streets of the town, bought polished rocks at a store on the main street, and swam in the pool at the Jerome Hotel. The day Mrs. Braden came downtown to take all the girls shopping was the one when I was dressed, along with the rest of them, in dirndls, complete with the white ruffled blouse, the flowered apron, and the round silver buttons. Happy as I was to be included, I also felt awkward and ill at ease, the tallest in the middle of a swarm of girls.

When Mummy arrived a few days later with Nick and Stewart, she kept the baby up with her at the cabin, and Stewart joined the rest of us downtown. Every other day or so, the grown-ups would gather the kids for a picnic and some trout fishing in the Roaring Brook. We'd perch in the grass on benches made from logs while Maria supervised, and the parents came by with fishing rods and posed for the camera, usually held by my mother. (I don't know what happened to Jimmy, but I suspect he'd been instructed to drive one of the cars back to California since Steve was returning to Harvard directly from Colorado.) On the picnicking days, I took Nick back from my mother and kept him out of trouble, eager to reassert myself in his affections. Mary Braden was fussing over her new baby brother, Tommy, who was only about six months old at the time, so there were two of us playing little mothers while our own mothers took their vacations. Mummy looked slightly frumpy and out of sorts next to Joan Braden who managed, even in outdoor clothes to look fashionably dressed, young and flirtatious. Whenever they're photographed together, Joan is smiling for the camera, conscious as she always was of her appearance, while my mother is looking away. That August, still on the wagon, Mummy had lost some weight, but in contrast to Joan's chic shorts, Mummy looked matronly in her orange skirt and sensible sneakers.

But I was happy for that month to be back in a pack, surrounded by other kids, out of the line of fire, away from our dark, brooding house. And then, suddenly, it ended.

Two weeks after we returned from Colorado, Ian left for Groton. For the next three years, I would be the oldest one at home.

DARK CORNERS

1960–1963

Recently, I told my husband that even though I loved dogs, I didn't want to own one.

"Is it because of the time the farmer shot Laddie?" he asked.

"I used to think it was. But now I realize I can't stand the idea of another beating heart in the house for which I am responsible."

After all these years, I still have that habit of waking from sleep, alert to any noise, my heart racing. My visiting granddaughter might cough once when she rolls over in her bed down the hall, but for the rest of the night, I'm the one who won't be able to go back to sleep for fear she will need me, that I will have to jump up and make things right.

Those three years when I was the oldest child at home, I listened to the house as if there were no grown-ups living there and I was the only one in charge. The fall Ian left for school, Stewart was eight years old, and Nick was fourteen months old. They both slept in rooms much closer to me than to my parents, who still firmly shut both hallway doors when they retired for the night. The maids upstairs must have known they were supposed to respond if they heard a baby crying, but their door was also closed. Mine was always cracked open.

In the fall of 1960, my mother was thirty-four years old. She had five living children and had lost several, including the stillborn baby boy. She was hanging on by a thread. But despite the family worries about her and her increasing depression, my father left in October for his usual fall reporting trip, this time to Africa. Because of the U.S. elections, which he couldn't work into long articles for *The Saturday Evening Post*, my father spent two months researching a piece on the political situation in

Africa for publication in the early spring of 1961. He traveled to the Congo, Nigeria, Togo, Guinea, Senegal, Kenya, and Ghana, and returned on December 22, a month after Kennedy's election. Soon after his return, he confided to Uncle Joe that he was worried about Tish, because even though he reported that she was trying so hard to be brave and good, she never enjoyed anything anymore.

Then slowly, the bottles came back into the house. I didn't see them, but her behavior gave her away. She began to smoke and twirl her hair again, those telltale signs that I'd learned to recognize as dangerous, even though I still didn't understand the cause.

One day, she might tell me that of course I could spend the night with my best friend Vicky, why did I even bother to ask? And the next day she might bark that I was seeing too much of that snotty little girl. It was like walking through a minefield, trying to decide where it might be safe to put my foot. She would hold Nick and coo over him as if he were still an infant while he struggled to get down. If I came upon them, I'd make up an excuse to lure him away, which only irritated her. Once she snapped, "You're not his mother, you know," and I left the room seething. *I might as well be*, I wanted to say, *for all the time you spend with him.*

Many nights, my father came looking for me in the house when he got home from his afternoon squash game.

"Where's your mother?" he'd ask.

"In her room."

A look of weary resignation came over him as he tromped slowly up the stairs to see what he would find behind the closed door, the one we knew never to open. Later, I'd hear him on the phone in the living room.

"This is Stewart Alsop. I'm so sorry to call this late, but my wife won't be able to attend the dinner tonight at the Embassy. She's not well. No, nothing serious. Yes, I'll be there."

And I'd spend another night attuned to the beat of the house while my mother stayed locked in her bedroom where, years later, we found the empty bottles rolling around under the bed.

❧

When the boys got home from Groton for Christmas vacation, Joe called a meeting of us oldest three in his bedroom. We put a sign on the door that foolishly read, TSCAP: TOP SECRET CLUB AGAINST PARENTS. Joe pulled some tape reels out of his suitcase, threaded them into the Wollensak recorder and pushed the play button with a look of triumph on his face.

The voices—all male—were faint, sometimes drowned out by the scrape of a chair or a phlegmy cough.

"What are they saying?" Ian asked.

"Just listen," Joe said. "They go through the list alphabetically so I'm one of the first." He rewound the tape. "Get closer so you can hear." He pressed the button again.

Scrape of a chair, some voices talking over each other, the name Joe Alsop, more muttering. When the main voice read out a second name, Joe switched off the machine.

"What is it?" I asked.

"The faculty meeting in Crocker's office. We bugged it. They're saying the night watchman reported finding me in the cellar under headmaster's residence."

We sat in awed silence for a minute. Jack Crocker was the Groton headmaster.

"Like the time we bugged Daddy's dinner party?" Ian asked.

"Right."

And my room. One night, before Joe left for Groton, he and Rich Bissell had run a wire along the roof between his room and mine when my best friend, Vicky, was sleeping over. As soon as I noticed the black line draped over the windowsill, I motioned to her to keep talking and crept along the roof to peer into Joe's room. He and Rich were hunched over a receiver listening to our conversation on headphones. Imagine their surprise when I yanked the wire and broke the connection before I scuttled back to my room.

I remembered this transgression when we had gathered around the tape recorder, but I said nothing. At least for this moment, we three were a team again.

"What were you doing in the cellar?" Ian asked.

Joe shrugged without answering.

With the help of Victor and Grenny, his two fellow conspirators, Joe had installed a tiny microphone in a bookshelf in the headmaster's office, so they could tape the monthly faculty meetings. That Christmas vacation, Joe spent much of the time in the basement building an amplifier so the voices could be transmitted more clearly. He refused to divulge any more details of the plan to Ian—I like to think it was for Ian's protection, should he ever be grilled under the lights. But I was just guessing. I knew nothing of their daily lives anymore. When the boys were away at school, they were completely gone from me.

In February of 1961, my uncle Joe suddenly got married to his best friend's widow, a thin, sophisticated American named Susan Mary Patten who'd lived in Paris for fifteen years. As usual, we children were not included in any of the plans for this event or even informed about it. From a photograph and newspaper clippings, I know where and when they were married, but little else. Bill and Anne, the two step-cousins who came with this marriage, stayed in their European schools until June, but in the summer Uncle Joe sent Anne up to our house in a taxi to spend the day with me. When the cab turned into our driveway, Anne remembers thinking that this couldn't be the right place. It looked like a haunted house. As I told her years later, it was.

Anne was a wonder to me. She looked foreign and chic with her jet-black hair, wide freckled face, and the bangs that tickled her eyelashes. My mother, ever sensitive to newcomers in this American land, gave her a pair of penny loafers to help her fit in, which endeared Anne to her forever. Even though this new cousin was a year and a half younger than me, she felt much more sophisticated, wise in the ways of the world and of men. And she set about teaching me.

In his bachelor days, Uncle Joe had entertained "Stewart's young" on Thursday nights, but now it was Anne I came to see. We endured the formal dinners at the highly polished table, and the increasingly heated political conversations between my uncle and his new bride and slipped away as soon as possible to Anne's basement bedroom, which had a convenient exit door through the garage. Nobody noticed when we snuck out and roamed the streets of Georgetown with no real purpose in mind just because we could do it. She taught me how to smoke without coughing and when she entered the sixth grade, unlike me, she really did need a bra. I broached the subject with Aunt Susan Mary, and without a word, she whisked us off to Lord and Taylor. For Anne, it was a humiliating trip simply because Susan Mary, in a loud French accent, asked the burly security guard standing by the revolving door if he could please direct us "to the *brassiere* department." It went downhill from there as the saleslady, to my aunt's amazement, kept having to go back to the stock room to produce larger sizes. Aunt Susan Mary clearly hadn't spent any time looking at her daughter's front, which is why I had to raise the subject to begin with.

Between my friend Vicky, whose sister taught us the facts of life, and Anne, my unofficial sister, I began to slide into a female world, away from the influence of the boys. I knew what a Kotex was used for even though it would be three more years before I'd need one. I got through dancing school classes without Ian because I fit in better, dressed finally in the stockings I bought for myself at Murphy's dime store. To be away from home was a relief because it meant I could let down my guard and not worry about where Stewart was hiding in the house, or whether Mummy was drunk and crooning over Nick, or snapping orders at the cowering maids.

Then suddenly, in the middle of April, Daddy went away with no explanation and came home with Joe.

I was standing at the door to my room, off the landing where the staircase took a turn, when I saw him starting up the steps.

"They caught you," I said in a low voice, as I could hear my parents in the hallway.

"I meant them to," he said defiantly. But of course, it wasn't true.

Joe with Victor and Grenny, his two comrades who'd bugged the headmaster's study, had gotten sloppy with the insider information until one day, Victor, who was listening on the headphones in his study, heard the masters discussing the possibility that the room was bugged. Jack Crocker sent a couple of prefects down to the fireplace hole, which he clearly knew about, and tested how much they could hear when he was talking. Victor alerted the other two who ran through the basement, tearing out the wiring, while Victor threw the headphones, the wire, and the tape recorder into the snowbank outside his window. In their panic, they'd torn the guts out of their system, which meant they'd cut themselves off from any information on the investigation.

"How did they get you, then?" I asked Joe that evening when the parents had gone out for dinner.

"Remember the night watchman who said he'd found me in the cellar? One day, walking into dinner, that guy was stand- ing by the door with a master and pointed me out. Then they searched my room, which was against all their rules. They'd already asked me all sorts of questions because Mr. Zinc, the science teacher, had said I was the only who could have pulled off something like that. We heard that on the tape. Anyway, they dragged me in for another interrogation, and I was still de- nying everything, and then they pulled out this sheet of paper with the plan on it."

"The wiring diagram?"

He nodded. "They found it in one of my notebooks when they went through my room."

"What did Daddy say?"

"He told Crocker all these stories about how he'd almost gotten kicked out of Groton for pretending to be a Baptist. Then Crocker took him down to the basement to show him where we'd run the wires."

"They left you alone in the headmaster's office?"

"Yes. Funny thing. I found they'd dug out the microphone I'd installed in the bookshelf. Daddy brought it home with him."

For years afterward, my mother kept the bugging device on her dressing room table in between a framed photograph of her brother Ian and a china bowl of her favorite pot-pourri. As a former decoding agent herself, she must have had a certain grudging admiration for her oldest son's achievement.

Joe didn't stay home for long. Within a matter of weeks, my father had refused to allow him to accept the invitation from MIT to attend college as a fifteen-year-old, and enrolled him in Manter Hall, a school for miscreants in Cambridge, Massachusetts. He moved in with John Kenneth Galbraith, a leading economist and diplomat and a good friend of Uncle Joe's, who agreed to house my brother for the two months remaining in the academic year.

With the personal hullabaloo going on at our house, I was only dimly aware of the Bissells' drama that same month. Mr. Bissell had convinced the new president to invade Cuba. The April 17 Bay of Pigs operation was a complete and embarrassing failure. Six months later, both Bissell and his boss, Allen Dulles, were forced to resign from the CIA. Like Joe, Mr. Bissell proved to be more adept at technology than at reading people.

As for me, when I wasn't trying to keep myself and my younger brothers safe, I was escaping to Anne's or Vicky's house. Boarding school began to look like a haven.

One spring evening, when I was in eighth grade, I showed up in my father's dressing room, a forbidden place I rarely visited without an invitation. Daddy looked surprised to see me but continued to brush his hair back from his face while leaning over slightly to see himself more clearly in the small upright mirror. It had already been decided that in the tenth grade that I would go to Miss Porter's, a girl's boarding school in Connecticut near where my grandmother and uncle lived. Now I can pretend that's why I decided to ask him and not my mother, but I know that's not the case. Her erratic behavior was the real reason I wanted to leave home early.

"Daddy, why can't I go to boarding school this coming fall?"

"Because we enrolled you for the tenth grade, not the ninth," my father said.

"I know. But why can't I go a year early?"

He looked mystified by my requests but didn't probe. Lots of questions in our house didn't get asked or answered.

After a moment, he shook his head. "Too late to change things now," he said, and with that, I was dismissed.

In those days, it would have taken nothing more than a phone call to the school administration to get me in for the ninth grade, but perhaps my father didn't want me to leave home yet. He must have known already that my mother was going to have another baby, and I'd proven helpful with the last one. Or more likely, he couldn't be bothered to deal with any of it—the school, my mother's reaction, or what it implies when your thirteen-year-old daughter begs to leave home.

The following January, I finally got a baby sister. I was fourteen when Alexandra was born: the perfect age to play little mother, the way I had with Nick, but now I was older and more experienced.

Alexandra had big ears and a little pug nose; she was a strong girl who at two-and-a-half months could already hold up her head without wobbling. I loved coming home from school to her gassy smile. I loved changing her diapers and washing her scalp while tucking her body securely under my left arm in what was known as the football hold. I knew how to keep her tummy pressed against my shoulder when she needed soothing, how to bump her pram over a sill to rock her to sleep. She slept on her stomach the way all babies did in those days as a preventive measure against crib death.

One day in late March of my ninth-grade year, I was called out of class to Reverend Mother's office. We girls rarely saw Reverend Mother, except to hold the door and curtsy when she swept past, the rosary clicking at her waist, the folds of black habit swishing with her step. Her dark-paneled office was dominated by portraits of the nuns who had founded the Order of the Sacred Heart, and the bookshelves were lined with leather-bound religious tomes. You only went to Reverend Mother's office if you were in trouble, and I couldn't imagine what I'd done wrong. I wasn't exactly a goody-goody, just a girl who was scared to bring too much attention to herself. Because of my experiences at home, I avoided minefields everywhere.

"Elizabeth, do sit down," she said in a kindly voice.

I sat and waited.

Reverend Mother took a deep breath. "I'm sorry to have to tell you, my dear, that Our Lord has gathered your little sister to His loving arms."

"Alexandra?"

"Yes. I just had a call from your aunt."

Alexandra whose diaper I'd changed this morning? Who'd wailed when I popped the bottle out of her mouth so I could burp her in the middle of her feeding? My baby sister gone to God?

"Let us pray together, my dear," she said, bowing her head. "Our gracious Lord, sad as we are at the loss of baby Alexandra, we are comforted by the sure knowledge that her sweet self has been gathered into your loving arms where, for eternity, she will never know pain or suffering. Amen."

I said nothing. I couldn't pretend gratitude when I felt confused and disbelieving, convinced that this would turn out to be a horrible mistake. Someone else's aunt had called. Someone else's baby sister had died.

Reverend Mother took me by the arm and introduced me to two strangers, a couple who'd driven out from Washington to enroll their daughter in the school. I sat in the back seat of their car, directing them in a robotic voice down Connecticut Avenue to our house. At the Rodman Street end of our driveway, I got out quickly and pretended to mount the steps to a neighbor's house so they wouldn't insist on taking me all the way to our kitchen door.

My father was away on a domestic reporting trip, but from the hallway I could hear my aunt Susan Mary making phone calls from his office. When I peeked around the living-room door, I saw a priest in black robes with his hand on my mother's shoulder, whispering to her. I couldn't see her face. Her body was motionless. I assumed they were praying.

It was finally clear to me that Reverend Mother had been telling the truth, but I wasn't ready to talk to anybody yet. More than anything, I wanted to say goodbye to my baby sister with nobody else there. I convinced myself that her small, neat body would be laid out on my parent's double bed.

Years later, when I tell my mother this story, she says in a gentle voice, "It's not surprising you thought she was there. Alexandra often slept in our bedroom. It was easier when I had to feed her at night."

This would only have happened when Daddy was away on a trip. He never allowed the babies to sleep in their bedroom.

That day, I crept up the stairs and down the long hallway, steeling myself for a still body wrapped in her receiving blanket, but when I finally got to the doorway, the bed was empty, the quilt stretched smooth by the maid.

I learned later that she'd been put down for a nap in her pram on the back terrace and when my mother went to check on her an hour later, she was dead. The fragile mosquito netting had blown over her body, but of course that wouldn't have stopped her from breathing. Her body went directly from my mother's arms to the ambulance to the morgue. The official cause of death was SIDS, or crib death, despite the face-down sleeping position recommended by the medical authorities at the time. Today, all young parents are told to make sure their babies are turned on their backs to sleep, but babies still die of this mysterious condition.

Alsops are buried in the Indian Hill Cemetery in Middletown, Connecticut. My father, away as he always seemed to be during a crisis, would have preferred Middletown for Alexandra, but my mother and Aunt Susan Mary, the ones on the spot, had to make all the tough decisions. Alexandra is buried in the infant's section of the Catholic Gate of Heaven Cemetery in Silver Spring, Maryland. I was the only one of her siblings who witnessed the lowering of her small coffin into the ground. My older brothers never even met her, as she was born after they'd gone back to school. It was decided that they shouldn't come down for the funeral, and that my younger brothers would find the graveside experience too upsetting.

The memorial plaque reads simply: ALEXANDRA, DAUGHTER OF STEWART AND PATRICIA ALSOP, JAN 4–MARCH 22, 1963. SUFFER LITTLE CHILDREN TO COME UNTO ME.

When, on a recent visit, I inquired about moving her body to the cemetery in Middletown so she could be near our parents, the officials in the front office told me as gently as possible that, by this time, there would be nothing left to move except the plaque. Dust to dust.

My summons to Reverend Mother's office was not unlike my mother's summons from dictation class at Carr Saunders Secretarial School to be given the news of her older brother's death in the Africa's western desert. Uncle Ian is buried in the Military Cemetery at El Alamein, Egypt, plot thirty-three, row G. The inscription reads simply: 2ND LIEUTENANT I. B. HANKEY, THE KING'S ROYAL RIFLE CORPS, 31 AUGUST 1942, AGE 20. FOR OF SUCH IS THE KINGDOM OF HEAVEN.

My mother, the obedient Catholic, conceived twelve children. Her first pregnancy ended in a miscarriage. (Mine did too.) Sometime after Nicky, she gave birth to a stillborn baby boy, a fact noted in Alexandra's birth certificate. Finally, after the birth of Andrew in her early forties, my mother applied to the local Catholic authorities for permission to have a hysterectomy, as her doctor had warned her of danger should she become pregnant again. She'd already survived two blood clots, one in her lung and another in her leg, both following pregnancies. After several months and many forms filled with intrusive medical questions, Cardinal O'Boyle, the archbishop of Washington, finally granted her permission to go ahead with the operation. From the age of eighteen to forty-two, she'd been continuously pregnant.

Not long after Alexandra's death, my mother left for two months in Greece with a good friend who was building a house on the island of Spetsai. While there, she wrote my father a letter that I read when I found the envelope on the hallway sideboard. After recounting the funny adventures of dealing with construction workers when neither she nor her friend Jane spoke Greek, she wrote: *Thank you for sending me the results of the autopsy report on Alexandra. I'm so glad to know that there was nothing I could have done to save her.*

As a child, I never witnessed the shape or size of my mother's grief. Many days, she kept herself away from us, and when she emerged, her feelings remained hidden behind a facade of efficient coping with whatever daily crisis the family generated. As a mother of two, I can now imagine more clearly what Alexandra's death must have meant to her. I'm sure I would have fallen apart. She never did, at least on the outside.

Nineteen sixty-three turned out to be a year of losses. In June, three months after Alexandra's death, my aunt Gussie, the wife of my uncle John, gave birth to a baby boy who died the next day. In early August, Phil Graham—a close friend of the family, and a man my mother once casually told me was in love with her—shot himself at their family farm in Virginia. Six days later, Jackie Kennedy lost her own baby, Patrick.

That summer, I spent a month with my cousin Anne at her mother's house on the coast of Maine. Standing in the snack bar line at the sailing club, I met the Princeton sophomore I was to marry seven years later. In September, on my fifteenth birthday, my mother drove me to Farmington, Connecticut, to start the tenth grade at Miss Porter's School.

I had escaped. Or so I thought.

PART III

The Downhill Slide

Escapes

I'm not sure whether my mother has Alzheimer's or, as the memory doctor surmises, alcohol dementia, but over time she has exhibited many of the classic symptoms of an Alzheimer's sufferer. For a while, she hid her small tapestry change purse full of dollar bills all over the house, convinced that somebody was stealing from her. If she couldn't find it, she'd accuse Zuni of taking it. When she began sending checks to every appeal, Zuni and Jan learned to sort the mail before they took it in to her. Her obsession with controlling the temperature in the house made us consider putting in a dummy thermostat, but we got through the hot summer with extra fans for Zuni. By the fall, she'd moved on to another obsession, one that has never abated...escaping.

In earlier days, when my mother was still able to take phone calls and make her own plans, Zuni came back one morning from walking the dog to find that Señora had left the house. The car was still in the garage, and Jan and another friend who often took her out for lunch had no idea where she was. Since she was on crutches and couldn't walk more than thirty steps at a time, we were confident that she wasn't alone. Zuni did eventually find a note saying she'd be home by three o'clock in the afternoon. She was having lunch with another friend who'd picked her up and returned her right on time. But I had this image of her scuttling down the street, a look of triumph on her face as she slipped out of the loving but intrusive grasp of her keepers.

I put out the word to all her friends that from now on, Zuni would keep the calendar and they needed to check everything with her before making a plan with my mother. The watchers are tightening the circle, and because my mother has been on crutches for fifteen years, we're pretty sure we won't have to worry about her getting too far.

But this week, Zuni calls to report that three times in the middle of the night, she's found Mummy by the front door without her crutches—the ones she's relied on for fifteen years. We are amazed that she can get that far by simply holding on to the wall, but it's nerve-wracking for Zuni, who's terrified that she will fall down the stairs to the basement.

I make the mistake of calling Mummy to recount what's happened. She has absolutely no memory of the sleepwalking and the fact that she can't remember agitates her more than the incident itself. Maybe it reminds her of blackouts during her drinking days.

We are on the phone for an hour while she asks me the same questions over and over again. When did this happen? How often? Where was I? What did Zuni do? Well, this is very disturbing because I can't do anything about it. We're going to take care of it, Mummy, I tell her. We'll get a monitor so Zuni can hear you more easily if you leave your room.

I have to make all the decisions now with the help of my brothers and the caregivers and mainly Jan, who's become a sister for me through this. But I hate this reversal of roles as does everybody who walks with an aging parent toward the exit sign.

I order a monitor to be installed in her room so Zuni can hear if she moves around at night, and a gate for the top of the stairs. When the man comes to attach the gate, Mummy sits in a dining room chair watching him drilling the holes for the screws, telling him it's for Morgan, the ailing corgi who sleeps in her room and never gets up in the night.

Lying on my back with my feet up the wall in yoga class, I feel a wave of sadness for my mother and all the things she has not been able to do for the last fifteen years with her increasingly crippled body. Her body betrayed her long before she lost her mind.

She has moved now to another country. I wish she could report back to me from where she is. More than thirty years ago, my father wrote a memoir called *Stay of Execution,* which tracked the progress of his leukemia. For all that he suffered physically, he knew what he was thinking and feeling each step of the way. He could remember what had happened to him yesterday, and a week ago, and he could envisage what was coming at him tomorrow.

Because he was tone deaf, Shakespeare was my father's music. When you walked upstairs in our house, you might hear the familiar phrases of a famous soliloquy issuing forth with the shower steam from under the bathroom door. When he crossed over into that "undiscovered country, from whose bourne no traveler returns," I could no longer receive his dispatches from the front. But, along the way, the man who had made his living as a journalist had been able to do what he'd always done: he reported.

My mother never really reported in, and now she can't. I feel strongly the loss of something I never had. I don't know if she understands the fragility of her condition, or whether her entire energy is now devoted to masking her insufficiencies. Is she aware that she's telling a bald lie when she announces to visitors that she still drives herself to the market every day? Or is it a desperate effort, despite all evidence to the contrary, to prove to herself that her life hasn't changed? Or is she simply asking us to nod and smile, to join in the charade so that she can feel she's still an independent person, in charge of her every move and decision while the circle of her caregivers, near and far, dance around managing her life for her just out of sight? Does it matter?

Will she go quietly into the next stage of this condition, or angrily, stubbornly, resisting every step of the way? This last is more likely considering the life she's lived. And who can blame her? A fierce refusal to accept the limitations of her arthritic body has kept her moving, despite all the years managing with crutches. When a few years ago, she lost her sense of taste and smell, she shrugged it off and kept insisting on eating good food and nurturing the plants in the garden room, all the while asking her guests, her caregivers, her children whether they could taste the cardamom in the stewed apricots or smell the jasmine in full bloom in the corner.

One of her favorite sayings has always been, "No point fussing." She doesn't complain, simply plows ahead, but I do not expect her to go gently into the days ahead.

The rage may not be pretty, but God knows, it is her right.

LINKS

In many ways, my life imitated my mother's. We both debuted at fancy dress balls, we were both married too young, we both "lost" our fathers in our twenties, and both of our first pregnancies ended in miscarriages. Like her, I attended a girl's boarding school, where I was thrilled to be away from the tensions at home, and where, once more, I was rewarded for being a good girl who never made trouble. Even though I slowly began to wake up at my politically radical college, I remained a timid follower of more outspoken leaders. The need to keep the peace and anticipate trouble so I could duck out of the way when necessary was deeply ingrained in me. So even though in later years I marched against the Vietnam War, I agreed in my freshman year at college to the round of parties and balls that made up a Washington debutante season.

I was eighteen, home from my first semester at college and sitting at my dressing table combing my hair, when my mother came to check on my progress. We were getting ready to attend the Cotillion, a debutante dance held every December at a local hotel ballroom. Although we debutantes wouldn't have to curtsy in one carefully orchestrated movement, as my mother had done at the Queen Charlotte Ball in London in 1943, I was wearing white from head to toe, including gloves up to my elbows. The unspoken assumption behind this WASP ritual was that this virgin was pure, available, and looking for a husband. And it never occurred to me to refuse to participate in this, or in the large party my parents threw the following June. But what I remember best about that moment was not the stunning teal-blue silk evening gown my uncle had ordered for my mother from his tailor in Hong Kong, but the way her belly preceded her into the room.

We locked eyes in the mirror.

"Not again?" I asked.

"Yes," she said, sinking down on to my bed. "The baby is due in May."

I was a freshman in college, and my mother was having a baby. My youngest brother was born that spring, and he's one of the reasons I was so experienced with babies by the time I had my own, but all I could think of in that December moment was "not again." From the look on her face, she was thinking the same thing. The twelfth pregnancy. How would this one go?

Both our first pregnancies ended in miscarriages. When the bleeding started for me, the doctor did a D and C—a procedure to clear the uterine lining—in a Washington office. Hers had been more dramatic with the doctor's late-night visit to the Pont Street flat in the middle of a V-1 raid.

When my college friends made plans to join the march on the Pentagon in my sophomore year, my mother suggested that a group of us stay at our house. Uncle Joe was outraged. A staunch supporter of the war, he told me angrily that we were young fools who couldn't possibly know what we were talking about because we hadn't seen "the secret documents." I pointed out that most of America hadn't seen the secret documents either, but he simply rolled his eyes and snorted at my naiveté. My father took a different tactic and interviewed us for an article. I remember my friends sitting on the Aubusson rug on our living room floor and answering the questions he threw at them while he scribbled notes. But I was playing a role in those years. Many of my classmates followed their convictions and joined radical organizations or went off to live in communes. Because I wasn't sure what else to do with my life or where to live, I got engaged.

Christmas vacation of my senior year in college, I was sitting with my parents in what we always called the big dining room when Daddy, in between bites, asked me when I was going to marry Peter, the boy I'd been dating since I met him at the age of fourteen while visiting my cousin in Maine. It was a casually delivered question, but behind it lay the not so gentle reminder that I needed to figure out what I was going to do after graduation, because we children were not welcome at home once we got through college. The nest needed to be cleared. This wasn't true for my two youngest brothers, because Daddy had died by then and my mother was more lenient with them, but we older four knew the score.

By that time, my college friends were making arrangements to room together in New York, and I hadn't been included in any of those plans because it was assumed that Peter and I would work something out. He was to graduate from architectural school the same month I finished Sarah Lawrence. That fall, I'd spent most weekends travelling from Bronxville, New York, to Princeton to help him build the balsa wood model of Manhattan's lower east side that constituted the thesis for his degree.

Responding to my father's question about marrying Peter, I said with a shrug, "I don't know. Maybe this summer." The previous fall, after some months away from each other, I'd met someone else and tried to break up with Peter. He'd been angry and upset. So even though we hadn't come to any formal arrangement, I knew he wanted to get married. I was the one who kept putting off the decision.

Such a hubbub ensued. My mother, looking alarmed, said, "That gives me only six months to plan the wedding."

It was decided that we should call Peter at home, and alert him to this happy turn of events. When I got through and told him what I'd done, he said, "Great," and immediately put his parents on the phone. Suddenly, everybody was congratulating everybody else. The two fathers knew each other, as Peter's father edited my father's articles for the Reader's Digest. It was, as they say, a marriage made in heaven.

I was the quietest person in the room, stunned at what I'd started. Maybe I was remembering Daddy's words from the wartime betrothal story. "Jesus Christ, trapped like a rat."

The wedding arrangements took on a life of their own. My mother, who'd had only five days to plan her own wedding, went into high gear. The former owner of our Springland Lane house had designed the living room to double as a ballroom. My parents gave a number of society balls in the 1950s and 60s as well as my debutante party in 1966, so my mother knew exactly who to call to have the furniture cleared and stored overnight, which florist could work best with the high ceilings, and how large a band could set up their instruments in the corner of the room.

I wouldn't be getting home from college until two weeks before the wedding, so the phone conversations with Mummy that spring revolved around lists and flowers and music and tents. In a single, small brave act, I said I wasn't going to be married in the Catholic church, which prompted my mother to make me promise not to have the ceremony in the National Cathedral; the Anglicans with their vestments and candles and occasional incense were close enough to Catholicism that she would consider it an affront. (Ironically, she hadn't objected when, in the third grade, I was selected to play the Virgin Mary in the annual Christmas pageant at the Cathedral.) Granny Hankey, who'd already shipped the family china from Gibraltar, told my mother not to give it to me unless I changed my mind and was married by a priest. I said no. My mother gave me the china anyway, and my grandmother refused to attend the wedding.

Naturally, the wedding was a Washington political affair. Besides the usual suspects from our widespread family and my parents' circle of friends—CIA agents, fellow journalists, and Congressmen among them—the list included prominent personalities from the Nixon administration. A photo of my cousin Alice Roosevelt Longworth and Peter's grandmother, descended from the Lees of Virginia, shows them smiling for the camera while any guests within earshot could hear them trying to outdo one another by listing their famous ancestors. Henry Kissinger's hang-dog face peers out at me from my own wedding album. Senator Edward Kennedy and his wife, Joan, sent us a platinum bud vase which Kennedy's secretary, mistaking us for constituents, had ordered engraved around the

base, To Walt and Liz, From Ted and Joan. (My husband's
legal name was Walter and Liz was the nickname I dropped in
the eighth grade.) The vase went to the thrift shop along with
three or four extra duck casseroles—the present of choice in
that bridal season—several ugly modern lamps, and not long
after, my wedding dress, which Mummy and I'd bought "off
the rack" for a very reasonable price. Although she let Uncle
Joe clothe her in gowns from his Hong Kong tailor, she didn't
believe in paying lots of money for clothes or getting sentimen-
tal about them, no matter how important the occasion. After
all, she'd been married in her tennis dress. The only piece of
clothing she brought to Washington from her childhood was a
long red-and-white-polka-dot dress with ruffles at the sleeves.
When we moved her from the old house to the new one, I
found this flamenco costume tucked into a box with two pairs
of castanets. She said I should give it to the thrift shop, but
without telling her, I stored it downstairs on a basement shelf.

My soon-to-be in-laws, who lived an hour away from my
college, were the only relatives who attended my graduation.
My mother was too busy with the wedding plans, and my father
said that the speaker, Margaret Meade, was a "pinko" which
was just his flimsy excuse to avoid any disruption to his normal
schedule. Although, looking back, I realize I was the only one
of the children whose college graduation they didn't attend, at
the time I accepted their excuses without complaint. The pattern was not a new one. My parents rarely appeared at any of
our school events, so here, on the eve of the big wedding they
were throwing for me, I didn't feel I could ask them to do more.

All through those days, I kept feeling that we were on an
unstoppable moving belt. A journal entry I wrote that spring
said, I'm marrying Peter in two months. I almost feel as if it's
happening to somebody else. I wonder if I feel about him the
way I ought to feel about the man you are going to live with the
rest of your life, but I don't know how to stop it.

One friend told me years later that she remembers me crying
when I hugged her in the receiving line, and another friend
recalled that I once said I had to marry Peter because I couldn't

believe that someone that good-looking, not to mention four years older, would ever be interested in me again.

These days, weddings seem to go on for ages. The bride and groom, married on a Saturday, usually show up at Sunday brunch and spend that day and even another with their remaining guests. In 1970, when I first married, that wasn't the case. Without telling me, my mother decided that we were hanging around too long at the reception, so she sped up the schedule. To my shock, just as I was beginning to enjoy myself, the photographer steered me into position so that he could get the obligatory picture of me stuffing a piece of cake into my new husband's mouth. Then my mother whisked me upstairs with the bridesmaids, who helped me change, and down I came again dressed in an embarrassingly short mini skirt. Under the barrage of rice and drunken cheers, Peter and I ducked into a cab that was waiting to take us to the airport. It was all over. I looked across the back seat at my new husband and burst into tears. I wasn't sure I'd done the right thing by marrying so young, and at that moment, my twenty-one-year-old self was furious that it was all over so quickly. My mother had ejected me from my own reception before I'd had any time to enjoy it.

Three years after she left England to start her new life in America, when my mother learned of her father's affair, she vowed she would never see him again. She kept that promise, although she did write to let him know when one of us children were traveling to England, so he could meet his only grandchildren. My turn came when I was touring Europe the summer I turned sixteen. Grandfather and I arranged to meet at Harrods for lunch, and I knew him the moment he walked into the reception area. A short man with a pinched, anxious expression, he was dressed in a bowler hat, a tweed jacket, and a bow tie. (My mother was five feet, nine inches tall, although of course now she's shrunk, but it seemed odd that she was so much taller than her own father.) He and I had no idea what to say to each other, but we fumbled our way through the meal and a polite visit to the department store zoo before he walked me to the bus stop. I remember looking down on him from my seat on the top deck of the red London bus and thinking, "That's my grandfather, who I'm sure I'll never see again." I never did.

By that time, he and his girlfriend, Clare, were living in Brighton on the English coast. He died in 1974 at the age of eighty-three, just weeks after my father succumbed to leukemia.

Surprisingly, for someone who could be so reserved and judgmental, my mother wrote to Clare soon after her father died and suggested they meet. Clare was delighted. Since my grandmother had refused to grant Arthur a divorce, the Hankey relatives had always made it clear that "Arthur's woman" was not to join him when he came for a visit or on the annual shooting trip to Scotland. Photographs of these "shoots" show him, still dressed in plus fours, standing a bit apart from the group, looking older and, if possible, more somber.

Through all the years she lived in America, my mother managed to get back to England every year or two when we children were young, and annually after my father died. Soon after Clare and she exchanged letters, Mummy took my two younger brothers with her to stay with her dear friend, Bee, in London and Cornwall, and it was then that they met Clare.

When she returned from that trip, she showed me a photograph of Clare with her hand on my youngest brother's shoulder. It seemed they'd all had a good time together, but after a second visit the following year, Clare broke it off. Apparently, Andrew, that same brother, then age thirteen, had neglected to write her a thank-you note for a Christmas present. Clare's letter, dated the end of January, brings up all her old grievances with the Hankey family and lumps my mother in with the rest of them. *It has become increasingly clear that neither you nor Andrew are in the least interested in me.*

My mother's response was remarkably measured and conciliatory: *I have _never_ regarded you with disdain. When my father chose to leave my mother and myself and spend his life with you, he broke my heart. Your decision to go with him had nothing to do with it.* She ends by saying *If you choose to keep in touch, I will welcome it, if you choose not to—I will understand.* Clare chose not to.

Here was one more abandonment for my mother. Clare's affair with Arthur had torn the Hankey family apart and destroyed the relationship with the parent Tish loved the best. And yet, my mother refused to blame Clare. I doubt I could have been that generous. Although Grandfather left my mother the bulk of his estate, and Clare promised in this last letter to *carry out your father's wishes*, my mother never saw a penny of the money, if in fact there was any.

My father died when I was twenty-six years old and pregnant with my first child. My mother last saw her father in 1946, on her first trip home to England as a married woman. The three remaining Hankeys celebrated her twentieth birthday in the little flat at 60 Pont Street. I wonder now if she ever regretted her stubborn refusal to meet with her father again. And on his part, I wonder if his life with Clare made up for all the losses connected with that decision.

War blows families apart in ways that are never recorded in the history books.

TURNING POINTS

Funny the way memory works. So much is lost and yet a movement, a Proustian scent, a sound, can freeze a moment into one
of the images in the slide show of your life.

I still remember that the phone in our apartment on Gram-
ercy Park South was ringing when Peter and I came in the door
from seeing *Klute*, a movie which I found deeply disturbing.

When I picked up the receiver, both my parents were on the
line, something that had never happened before. My heart sank.

"It seems, my dear," my father said in a gravelly voice, "that
my blood has turned to water."

At the age of fifty-seven, Daddy had been diagnosed with an
aggressive form of leukemia. Family lore holds that bad news
comes in threes. His mother had died the month before, and
his sister had recently undergone treatment for breast cancer.
The doctors at the National Institutes of Health gave him six
months to live but decided not to start treatment as there were
a few indications in the tests that his blood might be regen-
erating. It was the right decision. Over the next three years,
my father had more than one spontaneous remission. There
were days when he felt completely normal, when he wrote his
Newsweek column, played his afternoon game of squash in the
winter, tennis in the warm weather, and happily quaffed his
evening martini. And then there were other days when he had
no energy, sweated profusely through the nights, and when the
tiny cut from a fish bone could send him to the hospital with a
life-threatening bacterial infection.

We children visited more often, flying in from California,
New York, and even Nepal, where my brother Ian had settled
after a reporting trip to Southeast Asia with Daddy. At one
point, we all had our blood tested to see if we could give Daddy
platelets. Although my younger brothers Stewart and Nick were

both perfect matches, they were young, so until a better match was found through the national blood bank, Daddy's older brother Joe turned out to be the best option. We all joked that it would be hard to tell how much of our uncle's blood contained platelets and how much alcohol. And through it all, Mummy was the rock Daddy leaned on. During the years that he was sick, starting when four-year-old Andrew and eleven-year-old Nick were still at home, she rode the roller coaster from Spring-gland Lane to the hospital, and on weekends to Needwood, their Maryland house, where friends gathered to cheer Daddy up over bridge and a game of tennis. And in all that time, she picked up the bottle only once. Crisis stopped her drinking; it always had.

My husband and I had come down for a weekend visit a year after my father's diagnosis. The moment we arrived in Washington for the drive to the country, I could sense the tension in the house, from the Latina maids in the kitchen muttering to each other as they packed the provisions for Needwood, to my younger brothers hiding in their rooms, to my parents pretending they were glad to see us while speaking to each other in short, sardonic sentences. My mother was smoking, always a bad sign.

At some point during the interminable weekend, while we all avoided discussing the proverbial elephant in the room, my father asked me to take a walk with him down to the edge of the front lawn at Needwood. We leaned on the fence, staring at an enormous oak tree across the field while we spoke. Our eyes never met.

"Your mother is drinking again," he said in a low voice.

Although she wasn't in earshot, I could feel her watching us from the patio. I was twenty-four years old, and this was the first time my father had ever mentioned her drinking to me.

"I can't do this," he said. "I can't deal with the leukemia and her drinking. You have to do something about it. You have to speak to her."

I don't remember what I said. All I know is that by the time we got back to the house, he believed that he had shifted the problem to me and that I was going to fix it. He was fighting a disease that we all knew, deep inside, was going to kill him and I couldn't possibly refuse to do anything that would ease his daily life. I can admit now, all these years later, that I wanted to scream at him, *Who elected me as the family problem solver? This is your marriage. You're the grown-ups, I'm the child.*

But I didn't talk to my mother that day. I wrote her a letter, the coward's way out. I didn't know then all that I know now about alcoholism. I knew enough to say I loved her, but I hated the way she behaved when she drank. She wrote back, promising to stop. It wasn't an excuse, she explained, but the morning we were due to arrive, she'd woken up with a stomach flu and had mentioned it to Daddy. According to her, his response was, "Well, at least you don't have leukemia." That remark, after all the months she'd nursed and supported him, drove her straight to the bottle. In retrospect, I can't blame her, even though I know that alcoholics always find an excuse for their drinking. She didn't stop, although she never drank again during his illness.

In May of 1974, the family gathered at Uncle Joe's to celebrate Daddy's sixtieth birthday. He came out of the hospital for the party and spent most of the evening on the couch trying to talk, despite his compromised breathing. I was pregnant with his first grandchild.

When it was my turn to sit next to him, I said, "We're all pulling for you, Daddy."

Never a man to mince his words, he said, "Tell everybody to stop. I'm tired. I can't fight this anymore."

In his memoir, *Stay of Execution*, my father wrote, "A dying man needs to die just as a sleepy man needs to sleep, and there comes a time when it is wrong as well as useless to resist."

One week later, my mother called to say he'd slipped into a coma. When we children convened at the house, she cautioned all of us to think twice before going to the hospital. "Your father is in the bed and still alive, but he's not there. If you decide to go see him, be aware that this is an image of him that you might not be able to shake."

I chose not to go. When I think of my father now, forty-plus years after his death, he has ruddy cheeks, black hair, and that wry smile I remember from our discussions about writing or politics. If I'd seen him lying in that hospital bed with his spirit and his energy gone, I doubt I could ever have erased that picture from my memory.

My mother was forty-eight when my father died. Thirty years a wife, and as of this writing, thirty-seven years a widow.

When I visit my mother now, I fall into old behaviors. Instead of protecting my younger brothers from her alcoholic behavior, I try to protect the caregivers from her unpredictable explosions. She might yell at Zuni, who's trying to adjust her sweater. She might snap at Jan that she has no idea what we're talking about. She might slam her fist down on the table and yell at a dinner guest to shut up. Explosive, agitated, impatient, she once again unconsciously terrorizes the people around her.

She continues to be obsessed with getting out of the house. Even if she's just come in from a drive and had lunch, she wants to go out again. Since she can't drive anymore, I've hired people to take her for rides in the afternoon. Jan now drives her one afternoon a week to the birdseed store or along the canal to run Morgan, or to go grocery shopping. Zuni comes along, and they leave Mummy locked in the car with Morgan for company, while Zuni and Jan rush around the store, filling the basket as swiftly as possible. But Jan can't be available every day, and Zuni doesn't drive so the geriatric care manager feeds me names. In between the drives around the neighborhood, one lady, pretending to be working on a book, comes mornings to interview my mother on tape about her life. The afternoon home health aide takes her for drives when Jan is not available, but as often happens with dementia patients, the moment they get back home and my mother is comfortably seated in the garden room, she asks if they can go out. When I query my brother Joe about the money pouring out of the account, he tells me not to worry. Whatever it takes, he will cover.

When I'm there, I don't mind driving her around twice a day because it's the only time I know she relaxes, and there's nobody else in the car she can berate. It means I relax too. Getting out of the house is her version of wandering, a trait most dementia patients share. It must be infuriating to her that she can't just do it on her own. This is the only time that her restlessness seems to abate, and she stares out the window, commenting, as she always has, on everything. One time, it's the Halloween decorations, another time, the azaleas which turn the city into a spring arboretum.

We approach our old house on Springland Lane from the street below and park by the tennis court my parents built in the 1960s, which the current owners have restored. My mother lived in that house for fifty-three years, but as is her way, she hasn't shown much emotion about letting it go. Through the trees we can see the porch, which was tented for my wedding reception, and where for years we ate summer suppers, fanning away hordes of mosquitoes attracted by the smell of food and flesh. A section of that porch has been screened off to make a summer dining room, something we should have done when we lived there, but my parents had the same attitude toward their houses as toward their children: let things take their course and repair or intervene only when necessary.

"It doesn't look too different from down here, does it?" I ask.

"No."

The current owners had recently given my brothers and myself a tour of the renovated house. "They put in a circular staircase running up from the middle of our old kitchen," I tell her. "And they built a gym downstairs on the ground floor where Joe had his basement office."

"Good for them," my mother says. "They can do whatever they want. It's their house now."

End of discussion.

I turn around at the top of the dead-end street, but when I pull up at the light to make a left on Reno, she says, "Shall we go by the old house?" Sometimes, I say, "Sure" and we turn around. This time, I tell her we've just been there, and we press on. We have no particular destination on these rides, and because she forgets where we've been so soon after we've been there, I can take us around the same block ten times, and she gets the same pleasure out of the sights that she did just moments before. There's something to be said for the peace of living in each minute.

On this day, I tell her I'm writing about the time she and Daddy met at Allerton Park. I know this project of mine gives her pleasure, and when I bring it up, the relentless researcher in me is always hoping for one more tidbit. "Bee and I were down in the kitchen when he came in," she says in a dreamy voice.

"When who came in?"

"The one who was taking over."

My mind races to catch up with her. "The commanding officer?" I ask. "The one taking over Allerton for the duration of the war?"

"Air vice-marshal. Royal Canadian Air Force," she snaps impatiently, as if to say, what's happened to your brain?

"What were you doing in the kitchen?"

"Separating the honey from the combs. In marches Lady Mowbray with this man behind her, and suddenly she turns around and whops him on the arm with her pocketbook. She was absolutely furious at being turned out of her own house."

"What did he do?"

"Nothing. He just stood there and took it as if it was some sort of punishment he deserved. Then they passed right out of the kitchen and finished the tour."

We sit at another light in silence. I'm trying to think of a way to continue this conversation while keeping all these details in mind until I can get home to write them down.

"What did Lord Mowbray have to say about it?" I ask as the light changes.

"Who?"

"Lord Mowbray, Bee's father."

"I have no idea," she says, but I can tell by the change in her voice that the moment of clarity is over and she's no longer sure who Lord Mowbray is, never mind Bee or even me. I think she knows I'm her daughter, but she might not remember my name in that moment. As I think about it, I realize she hasn't said my name in a long time. She simply calls me, "dear" or "love."

We drive on as I wonder to myself why Lady Mowbray was carrying her pocketbook on that house tour. I've been following my nose as my mother used to say and haven't been paying too much attention to where we're going. We're on the far side of Georgetown on a busy road I don't recognize.

"Do you know where we are, dear?" she asks suddenly.

"Actually, Mummy, I don't. But I have one of those mapping things on my phone so don't worry, I can get us home."

"Go down to the next light and take a left," she says in a confident voice. I think, what the hell, if she gets us more lost, it doesn't really matter.

She guides me home, telling me when to put on my signal, and which lane to get into, the kind of instruction that used to make me irritable. But, for this small space of time, I rejoice. My mother is back, the one I had between the drinking and the dementia.

My mother stayed off the bottle through my father's funeral, the flight up to Middletown, Connecticut, with the casket to bury him in the family plot, and even through the airing of the interview he'd done with Dick Cavett, which was shown a month after his death.

That summer, as was our custom, my husband and I spent an August week with her and my younger brothers in a seaside house that good friends lent to my parents for a month every summer. I was seven months pregnant but feeling fine. My mother seemed calm, and from all reports, she hadn't picked up a drink since Daddy's death.

The day started off well. The sun was shining, and when the morning breeze picked up at midday, my husband, an experienced sailor, and my brother Nick's fifteen-year-old friend Raymond decided to go out on the sunfish, one of the fleet of small boats that had been put at our disposal. They skimmed across the water until they were halfway to the Connecticut shore, but when they tried to come back, we could see from the shore that they were having trouble. Suddenly the mast snapped off and they were being swept out to the open ocean with no way of maneuvering or steering the sunfish. A fishing boat rescued my husband and brought him back to shore to call for help. For some reason, nobody thought to tow Raymond back with them, so he continued to drift. That's when Mummy and I made the foolish decision to go after him in the rowboat.

I started out rowing, but we were going against the wind, and after about twenty minutes, I began to feel strange, unfamiliar ripples across my belly.

When I told Mummy, she looked alarmed. "Contractions?" she asked.

"Maybe."

"Let's switch," she said. "I'll row for a while."

And then, even though we were experienced in boats and knew how not to behave, we did absolutely the wrong thing and both stood up at once. Suddenly we found ourselves in the cold salt water, clinging to the hull of the rowboat. One oar was still trapped in the lock while the other floated away with the current.

"Should I go after it?" I asked.

Mummy shook her head. "We're going to kick to shore," she said.

Strange as it is to say, that was the most intimate and familiar moment I remember with my mother. Buried somewhere in the family photo albums, there is a picture of us in the pond at Polecat. She floats on her back in one inner tube, her short hair curling over her earrings and her feet tucked under the rim of my inner tube, steering me in for a landing. Two decades later we found ourselves, once again in the water. We were both soaking wet, both worried I was going to give birth two months early, but laughing at the absurdity of our situation as, side by side, we kicked our way against the current toward a string of rocks that jutted out from the shore. Raymond had become a small dot on the horizon, straddling his board and waving for help. The day was clouding over, but the air was still warm as the breeze had died down a bit. We chatted about the birds, about how much more you could see of the big houses from out here on the water, about the approaching clouds and whether they carried rain, all the while battling the current, which seemed to be dragging us bit by bit across the Long Island Sound to the opposite shore. This was a crisis of sorts, but one we'd created together with our silly notion of rescuing Raymond, and neither one of us was panicking. I was used to how dependable my mother was in a crisis, whether it meant burying our dead beagle in a makeshift grave or holding my father together during the worst of his hospital stays, but here I was next to her, just as calm. Drawing courage, one drew strength from one another in our ridiculous situation. And finally, we managed to propel ourselves close enough to catch hold of the very last guano-covered rock on the jetty we'd been aiming for.

We got home to find my husband had called the Coast Guard, and Raymond was being towed into the beach. We were all laughing and comparing notes when suddenly Mummy walked out of the kitchen carrying a bottle of white wine.

"After that ordeal, I think we all deserve a drink," she announced in much too bright a voice, and for the first time in front of her family, she poured herself a glass of wine. We all froze, took our seats, and looked the other way.

How ironic that the bubble of my intimate moment with her was popped so quickly after we got home.

After that, the drinking didn't stop. It got worse. In addition to the vodka bottles probably still hidden under her bed, she now raised her wine glass at dinner parties and ordered a cocktail whenever a host asked for her drink selection. She smoked in public, and her voice grew loud and abrasive. The invitations from old friends dropped off, and she blamed them for abandoning her after Daddy died. When my daughter was born in October and she was supposed to come help, she sounded drunk on the phone when I called from the hospital.

"I have an awful cold," she said. "I don't think I'd better come right away, dear."

"I agree, Mummy," I said, hugely relieved. I had no idea what I was going to do with a brand-new baby in one bedroom of our small apartment and my mother drunk in the other. Two days later, I got a call from a friend of hers demanding to know why I'd refused to let my mother come to see her first grandchild. That's the way with drunks. They're always revising history, explaining away their behavior, blaming the other person.

For the next two-and-a-half years, she was pretty solidly drunk. Even though I felt for her as a young widow, I avoided visiting as much as possible.

My second pregnancy was unplanned and complicated. I protested when the doctor told me I was twelve weeks pregnant.

"I had a period six weeks ago," I said.

He shrugged. "These things happen. My first Copper-7 failure," he added with an odd note of pride in his voice.

Well, then you have the baby, is what I felt like telling him. We'd wanted a second child, but the timing was off. It was decided that the IUD should be left in to avoid the possibility that removing it would cause a miscarriage. Then three months later, I started to bleed. In those days, nobody did regular ultrasounds. When I called from Rhode Island to discuss my situation with the midwife at the hospital, she told me that I was probably miscarrying.

"Lie down, take care of yourself, and come see us when you get back to New York."

I returned to the city some weeks later, assuming I'd lost the baby.

They found a heartbeat and finally sent me for an ultrasound. The radiologist was the one who told me that I'd been carrying twins and had lost one.

"I see this all the time," he said. "Women conceive twins more often than we think."

The dates were adjusted. I'd been six weeks pregnant, but with two, not one. I must have been in touch with my mother in those months, but I have no memory of that time except for the exhaustion of caring for a two-year-old while worrying about the second baby who was sharing my womb with a foreign Y-shaped plastic object. The IUD had eliminated one fetus. Would this second one come out damaged or missing some vital part? If Mummy hadn't been drowning her despair in the bottle, would I have been able to turn to her for advice and support? After all, she'd had so many miscarriages, a stillborn baby boy, a little girl who died. She might have been a comfort for me that year, but I doubt I would have turned to her, even if she'd been in one of her dry periods between binges. I'd always believed I had to solve my own problems. It was a habit that would take a lifetime and the love of a good man to break.

My fourth brother, Nick, was away at boarding school that winter, but one evening in February, close to my delivery date, my youngest brother, the one who'd been born when I was a college freshman, phoned collect from the maids' room on the third floor. When Andrew was four, Daddy had been diagnosed, and when he was seven, our father died. Nine years old that January, Andrew was the only child still living at home. He'd broken his leg and because the plaster cast covered his knee, he couldn't get up the steps of the school bus. Mummy was supposed to drive him to school. Apparently, every morning she would emerge from her bedroom to tell him he couldn't go to school that day because he'd had a terrible asthma attack the night before. It was the maids who'd urged him upstairs and demanded he call me.

"I don't remember having asthma last night," he said,

sounding bewildered. "She's in her room all day long. We barely see her."

She was giving herself a reason not to drive him to school because it was pretty clear that she'd been on the booze for a solid month and might well drive him into a tree.

I called my cousin who lived nearby. We'd turned to her before to deal with Mummy, so I'd been reluctant to lean on her again, but suddenly, I couldn't stand it anymore. I didn't want to give birth to my second child worrying about my little brother, alone in the minefield with nobody but two sweet, but barely literate, Spanish-speaking maids to protect him.

"I'm on my way," she said. "Why didn't you call me earlier?"

She went over, packed Andrew's bags and schoolbooks, and moved him into her house. My contractions started, but I was still home when she called to report.

"Your mother is in terrible shape. She's seeing little green men coming out of the walls."

"She wasn't locked in her bedroom?"

"No, she came down the stairs when Andrew and I were leaving, but she barely recognized me. She was having the shakes, delirium tremens."

"That means she's taken the Antabuse. That's the way she stops the binge. It makes her hideously sick. Where are Olga and Nora?"

"Cowering in the attic," she said. "We can't leave your mother there in that condition. I've called Uncle Joe and he's getting her a bed in the drying-out wing of Georgetown Hospital."

"I bet he had to pull a lot of strings for that bed," I said, my sense of humor intact despite the contractions.

After that, I concentrated on having a baby. My son Andrew, named after his nine-year-old uncle, was born on a Sunday. The afternoon before, my cousin and Uncle Joe had met the ambulance at our house. Raymond, who lived up the street, followed the siren down our driveway and witnessed my mother being carried out of the living room door in a strait jacket. Years later, my mother said, "I didn't mind Raymond seeing me that way, but I know the nosy neighbor down on Springland was also watching. That made me furious."

Sorry, Mummy, I thought. *Drunks don't get to choose their entrances and exits. You gave up that right a long time ago.*

Monday morning, Uncle Joe called me on the hospital phone.

"Darling," he said, "we've gotten your mother into Georgetown, but you have to come down this afternoon because we have to arrange to move her into rehab by Tuesday."

"Uncle Joe," I said calmly, "I had a baby yesterday."

"Good for you, darling. What kind of baby?"

"A boy."

"Excellent. Well then, you can come tomorrow."

I laughed and told him to call one of my brothers. I was determined to lose myself in motherhood, and at that point, I wasn't sure how long it would be before I could stand to spend any time with my own mother. She'd abandoned me as a child, and now, when I could have used her help more than ever, she was gone again. A wall went up between us. At least, I was aware of one. It took her longer to notice.

After a month in the rehab and some counseling and Alcoholics Anonymous meetings, she never drank again.

Every year on my son's birthday, I'd call to congratulate her. "Mummy, you've been sober five years. Ten years." And every year she'd remind me that, when she saw my cousin taking her youngest son away from her, she'd swallowed the Antabuse which, after a month-long binge, made her violently ill. She'd been warned that the side effects of mixing the drug with alcohol include low blood pressure, vomiting, sweats, fast heartbeats, and chest pain, but it was the only way she could get herself to stop. I've never said that my mother isn't a courageous woman.

She went to AA and sponsored several people, including a disastrous young woman named Jane whom she moved into my old bedroom. She lent Jane money that never got repaid, a car that Jane wrecked, and gave up hours she could have spent with Andrew listening to Jane's troubles. I used to think of Jane as her replacement daughter, her way of making up for my lost childhood. Finally, when Jane started drinking again which threatened my mother's sobriety, Mummy threw her out.

When I visit my mother these days and am met by that blank stare from her "throne" in the garden room, I'm reminded of a comment she made to me some years after that final binge, when she was carried out of the house in a straitjacket.

"What took you so long?" she asked one day.

"What do you mean?"

"What took you so long to get me out of that bedroom?"

I exploded inside. *It's my job to get you to stop drinking? I'm the child here. It's your job to take care of me.* Does every child of an alcoholic feel this inchoate rage at the suggestion that they are the ones who should be taking action to fix the problem? As usual, I turned away and didn't answer. The mines in the field were still live. I couldn't afford to step on one.

I think of that comment now as she watches me bustle about the room, straightening the magazines, while I try to fix on a topic of conversation she can follow. Is she wondering what's taking her daughter so long to get her out of this predicament, this brain fog that has crept up on her and doesn't seem to be getting better?

I'm doing my best, Mummy, I say to myself instead of to her, *to make sure you feel safe and comfortable and cared for. From a distance. I rely on others to feed you, dress your wounds, keep you clean, put you to bed. The care is there, but so is the distance. It's the best I can do.*

After the beagles, my younger brothers got to pick the dogs. In 1966, when Him, one of President Lyndon Johnson's beagles, was hit by a car while chasing a squirrel, the White House was inundated with replacement dogs. LBJ sent a Boston bull terrier over to our family in a White House limousine. It was seven-year-old Nick's turn for a dog, but the black and white terrier was hidden in the basement until Christmas morning when, as was our tradition, we children trooped into the living room to view our presents. Nick was so overcome with excitement that he couldn't think of a name for the puppy, so Daddy christened him Nemo. (LBJ had the same problem choosing dog names. One early dog was called simply Beagle and the pair he brought to the White House, Him and Her.) Andrew's choice was a long-haired dachshund named Foxy. Once all the children had left home, my mother returned to the corgis of her British childhood. First was Puma, who seemed to have been named after a sneaker, and then her final dog, the one she calls Morgan in honor of his Welsh breeding line.

Children make Morgan anxious; he shares that with his mistress. When grandchildren come to visit, we put Morgan out in the garden or lock him in my mother's bedroom. Now that he's aged and become more sedentary, he can be trusted to stay in the garden room with visitors as he simply resorts to a warning growl if a toddler gets too close.

Morgan is totally imprinted on my mother which makes ~~him happy. He's chosen for her all the homes that run our own. He~~ knows her pace, every clink and thump of the crutches. He's taught us to go on ahead of her the way he does, so as not to embarrass or rush her by sniffing at her heels. He's comforted by the way she whistles during her slow march down the hall, while we understand she uses the melody to divert a visitor from the sight of a woman, bent double, more crab than human. He waits for the rattle of the scoop in the kibble barrel, but when she forgets and collapses with relief into her chair, he barks an order. She tells him to hush, sometimes in Spanish, but he keeps on barking until she struggles back to standing, feeds him, lets him out and then in again.

Morgan marks time for my mother, watches over her, announces visitors, patrols the hallways, frightens the plumber, the would-be intruder, and the family of rats who live under the back steps. He bustles about the house when she no longer can, sneezing at dust in the corners, lapping up water from the plant containers so Zuni can do her job and refill them. At night, he leads the way to bed, sees my mother safely in, falls asleep on his padded pillow to the hum and bubble of TV voices, the click of pill bottles, and her murmured prayers.

I want her to go first, but it's not to be.

Yesterday, Jan called to report that Morgan's had a couple of seizures. He's now on meds three times a day, and Zuni is running two pill boxes. He sleeps a lot, has not much appetite, and moves slowly. My mother has always hated anything wilting in the house. She demands that flowers or plants be thrown out the moment they show the first sign of decay. Now she calls Jan daily to see whether it's time to put Morgan down.

When I speak with Mummy about him, I point out gently that Morgan isn't suffering, he's just slowing down and sleeping more. I might as well be talking about her.

The vet suggests an MRI to determine whether Morgan has had a stroke, but my oldest brother and I say no. If the medications are working and he's not in pain, why bother? Just keep him comfortable. Are we practicing for the moment when we might have to make that kind of decision for our mother?

The day comes. It's unfair to put it off any longer.

Morgan's started dragging his back legs behind him, and has been messing himself and the rugs. These last weeks have been hardest on Zuni, who's had to clean up after Morgan and figure out how to walk him, but it's clearly depressing my mother to watch the last of her dogs die a little more each day.

Jan, Zuni, and Mummy all go to the vet together. Once Dr. Murphy has examined Morgan one more time, she kneels in front of Mummy to explain that there's nothing more she can do for him.

"It's time for him to go, then," my mother says, a question really.

Dr. Murphy nods. "I'll give him a shot to put him to sleep," she says, "and a second one to stop his heart. He won't feel a thing. Would you like to hold him while he goes?"

My mother shakes her head.

"Would you like to have his ashes?"

My mother shakes her head again. I can almost hear her thinking, "What am I supposed to do? Bury him in the garden so I can look at his grave all day? What nonsense."

When the vet carries Morgan out to the waiting room so that they can all say goodbye, my mother finally starts to cry. She kisses his head, then Zuni and Jan whisper their own goodbyes. And it's over.

The first few days after Morgan goes, my mother asks her customary, "Is the dog out?" Only at night, as she's headed to bed, when Morgan used to take the lead down the hallway, does she say to Zuni, "You and I miss him the most, don't we?"

And Zuni agrees. In the darkening house, one of the beating hearts has stopped.

A few days later, my mother no longer remembers him.

TELLING THE TRUTH

Zuni calls to report that my mother is weak and has congestion in her chest. The exercise therapist emails that Tish seems vacant, depressed. The nurse who visits twice a week tells me she was shocked by how quickly my mother appears to have gone downhill. All three calls within one hour.

I mobilize. Calls to the nursing agency, the doctor, Jan. Emails fly. By two o'clock in the afternoon, we have a licensed practical nurse in the house for twelve-hour shifts. The physician's assistant arrives the next morning dispatched by the doctor who finally understands that I want my mother treated at home no matter what that takes. The mobile x-ray unit comes to the house.

Of all things, she is diagnosed with asthma.

I have asthma, my father had it, my great-great uncle Theodore had it, my brother and nephew and granddaughters all have it. But never my mother. The treatments are familiar to me. Nebulize her with Albuterol, administer Flovent to open the passageways. The physician's assistant explains that with the peculiar weather we've had on the East Coast, there has not been a frost all winter in Washington and the pollen counts are very high. "We have seen elderly patients develop asthma in their eighties," she tells me.

It doesn't seem fair that my mother must add this to a long list of other complaints. She can't smell or taste, she can barely walk and only with crutches, she has a sore on her back that might be a yeast infection, she is always cold, her brain is shrinking daily so she gets no pleasure from reading or television and can no longer play bridge. She's sick to death of looking at her garden. Welcome to old age, which one of my uncles termed a shipwreck, while another always said it "ain't for sissies."

She doesn't like the nurse in the house, fights her at every turn, Zuni reports. I don't want to witness this. I am so grateful that we have enough money and I've set up enough systems, so I don't have to be there.

Besides that, I'm pretty sure she doesn't want us to see her this diminished.

Two weeks ago, when I was visiting, I suggested we drive past her first house in Georgetown, the one she and my father bought in 1946. She loved the idea, but steadfastly refused to have me push her to the car in the wheelchair, help she'd been accepting and asking for in the last few weeks from the care-givers. One painful step at a time, she walked from the chair in the garden room to the car, the distance of a football field, which meant that she was breathing heavily once we got into the car. By the time we'd reached Georgetown, she'd started to cough, and she couldn't stop. That juicy cough that she couldn't control embarrassed her, especially in front of me.

People marvel at what a wonderful system I've set up to take care of her at home. I'm not holy. I'm simply making sure that I put in enough layers, so I'm not called upon to attend to her and interrupt my life once more for her needs when she had so little time for mine. I don't want to witness her naked rudeness to the people around her, the imperious behavior that the brain disease has revealed now that the British graces and politesse have been stripped away. Drinking used to do the same to her, and I can't bear to watch that again. The little girl inside me is screaming to be protected. Scar tissue grows over the childhood wounds, but clearly it doesn't take much to re-open them.

On one of my regular trips to see my mother, I tell her I'm visiting a friend, when I'm actually out with Jan touring an as-sisted living place with an Alzheimer's floor. We come away de-termined never to put her there. I research nursing homes and find only one that isn't a franchise. When I come in from one of these secret forays, she greets me, pleased, not remembering

I was there that very morning having breakfast on a tray in her room. When she wakes up tomorrow, I'll be a welcome surprise all over again.

It's so hard to talk to her now because I miss who she used to be. She repeats herself all the time, asks the same questions three times in one conversation. She knows her memory has fallen off a cliff, but in the moment, she doesn't remember that she doesn't remember. As always, she has comments and opinions on everything, which continues to be her way to stay in the conversation, but she generates almost nothing.

And then suddenly, with no warning, she surprises me. We are sitting in the garden room as usual, when she asks out of the blue, "When do you think I became an alcoholic?"

"I don't know, Mummy."

"I mean when did you first notice there was something wrong?"

"My friend Vicky and I had a code. If things were bad at our house and you were in the living room when I was talking to her on the phone, I'd ask to borrow her tennis racket. Pretty silly code when you think about it. I mean why would I need her tennis racket in the middle of the winter?"

For once, my mother is like a dog with a bone and doesn't get distracted by my extraneous comments.

"What else?" she asks.

"Ian and I used to meet in the kitchen after school. He came in first, so he'd let me know where you were and what mood you were in. We thought you had some kind of mental imbalance. We talked about schizophrenia, but we didn't know what it was."

"You didn't know I was an alcoholic?"

"How were we supposed to know? You never drank in front of us."

"When did you find out?"

"I remember the exact moment. It was when I was a freshman in college, and Ian had come down from Dartmouth to go to a party with me in New York. He told me while we were waiting in line at a deli to buy ice."

"How did he find out?"

"He finally asked Daddy, who was shocked we didn't know."

"I guess your father thought you would discover my secret by osmosis," she said. "I always assumed he would have told you all at least by then. Good for Ian for asking."

There's a pause before she returns to the original question. I wonder if she's forgotten that she asked it a few minutes ago.

"When do you think I became an alcoholic?"

I'm tempted to hold back, but I don't.

"I met Vicky at Stone Ridge in the fourth grade. So, at least from when I was nine until I was twenty-eight years old, and my son Andrew was born. Nineteen years. And maybe before that. I don't know."

She looks as if I slapped her in the face. But she's asking and I'm not going to fake my answers to soften the blow. I'm long past that. And I'm sure we won't get another chance to have this conversation.

"You children and your father had to put up with it for so long."

I nod.

When I joined Alanon—the program for relatives of alcoholics—in order to help me understand the drinking disease and my part in it, I learned that the eighth step asked the alcoholic to make a list of all people she had harmed. Step nine suggested the alcoholic make amends to those people except when to do so would harm them or others. Although my mother went to AA after rehab and sponsored other alcoholics, both formally through the program and informally through personal friendships and connections, this moment in the garden room is the closest she'll ever get to that formal ninth step. She has never looked me in the eye and said, "I'm sorry for all the pain my drinking caused you." And she doesn't do that now. But in that one sentence, she acknowledges that it was a lot to put up with.

"What was it like for you?" she asks.

"Like walking through a minefield," I tell her. "I never knew what mother I would find when I came home from school.

That's why Ian waited for me in the kitchen. To give me the thumbs-up or the thumbs-down sign. You did that thing where you constantly curled and uncurled your hair, ran it back and forth through your fingers."

"Your father hated that."

"You smoked when you were drinking. I came to connect the smoking with your scary moods."

She absorbs all this.

"I think it tipped over," she says thoughtfully, "when I worked with Annie Bissell at the hospital, and we spent those afternoons with the vodka bottle around her kitchen table. I'm not blaming her, but that's when I became an alcoholic. It creeps up on you."

"What about your family in Gibraltar? Did they drink?"

"Not much. My uncle Wilfred was a drunk, but he'd been through some of the worst battles of the First World War and came home with ruined lungs, so nobody blamed him. Every so often, my parents had a cocktail. My mother only drank sherry."

We let the words swirl around the room and float away. The squirrels and birds on the feeder distract us briefly. Then she speaks again.

"When I went to that drying-out place, Silver Hill, the first counselor I had put it to me bluntly. 'You're an alcoholic,' he said. I was shocked. I couldn't believe it. But then, after three days, he pushed off and the second person wasn't any good. When I left there, I thought I'd beaten it. But years later, after your father died, I needed a second round of treatment at Melwood. Jim, the counselor there, said, 'Well no wonder you're an alcoholic. You've had so much loss in your life.'"

She snatches a Kleenex from the box, blows her nose. Her eyes are glistening with tears. I don't mention it and neither does she, but she cries quietly through the next few minutes.

"You did have so much tragedy," I say. "Your brother dies, your father abandons your mother, and you leave your whole life behind to come here. Not to mention what you went through in London during the war."

"And the men," she says. "You'd have dinner with a fellow Saturday night, and he might be dead the next week."

No wonder you hate hellos and goodbyes, I think. She snatches another Kleenex, blows again.

"And nobody here in America really knew what you'd been through. Or cared."

"That's right. For a while I was like the Edward R. Murrow report from London. They were interested briefly in my experiences, but it was nothing more than a story to tell at a party. After a while, nobody wanted to hear it anymore. They wanted to move on. Especially the women."

"Were they jealous of you?"

"Yes. They hadn't lived through it the way I had. If there were a soldier in the room, I'd end up talking to him, comparing notes. The women didn't like that."

When Zuni comes in with my mother's morning drink of Boost, my mother wrinkles her nose. Most of it will be left in the glass.

This interruption has flipped the memory switch. We've said all we're going to say on this subject.

Coming Together

In the summer of 1978, while staying at my in-laws' Rhode Island beach house, I discovered I was pregnant, again unplanned. I knew instantly that I couldn't possibly handle a third child. I was working on my second young adult novel, the one about two boys who discover after their father dies of a blood disease that their mother is an alcoholic. I hadn't told anybody in the family what I was writing, least of all my mother. The novel was pouring out of me and I didn't want to stop the flow. Looking back now, I think it might have been the first time I stood up for myself and said, no. I will not do this. I will not be the good girl who goes along.

Luckily for me, within twenty-four hours of conceiving a baby, my mouth always tasted like the inside of a metal post, so the local gynecologist agreed nervously to do an abortion since, as he put it, I was only two weeks "gone." Fearful of protesters, he cautioned me several times to tell anybody who asked that I'd had a D and C procedure. My husband said he couldn't come up from his job in the city, so his aunt drove me to the office and home again and put me to bed. All seemed fine.

Three days later, I took the children, one aged three and the other five months, to the island to spend our customary August vacation with my mother. Newly sober, she presided over the usual household, which included Andrew and Nick, both with friends, and Olga and Nora, the Salvadorean maids who would take care of my children while I worked on my novel in a small room over the garage. There was no way I was going to tell my mother about the book while I was writing it. If it was accepted for publication, I'd deal with it then. If it wasn't, I'd bury it in a desk drawer and move on.

The night I arrived, I began to bleed, first a dribble and then by midnight, a flood. Terrified as I always was to disturb my mother in the middle of the night, I tried to staunch the blood with napkins and then towels, until finally I had to admit I needed help and knocked on her bedroom door.

"What's wrong, dear? Is it one of the children?"

"No, it's me. I'm bleeding."

"Good lord," she said, as she spied the trickle of blood running down the inside of one leg. She led me back to her bathroom. "What happened? Did you have another D and C?" She was remembering my first miscarriage only six months after my wedding day.

I took a deep breath. "I had an abortion, Mummy. Four days ago, in Rhode Island."

I will never forget the look of shock on her face. This devoted Catholic woman—who, despite the threat to her own health, had refused to have a hysterectomy until the archdiocese granted her permission—had birthed a daughter who'd just admitted to committing what was, in her eyes, a mortal sin.

The silence seemed to last forever while I sat on the toilet dripping blood into the bowl. Did it cross her mind in that moment that if she'd had choices like that, she might have led the life she wanted, not just the one her body and her church imposed on her?

"I'm not lying to you anymore," I said. "And I don't regret the decision. There's no way my marriage would have survived another child."

She didn't say anything. There were no recriminations. She simply tucked me into bed, got the island doctor to do a home visit, and in a few days the bleeding stopped. I went back to work on my novel about the alcoholic mother in the room over the garage. I wasn't going to lie anymore, but I also wasn't going to tell the whole truth until I was ready. In fact, she never knew about the second abortion or finally, the tubal ligation with its own complications. I don't think either of those decisions would have shocked her. By that time, she'd been a sober widow for five years and had set about reclaiming her own life, the one she'd had to put on hold when she married an American soldier at the age of eighteen.

∾

We became friends, but the ride wasn't smooth.

My uncle John used to say that "every time Elizabeth writes a book, it's like dodging a bullet." In the fall of 1978, I published *Knock Knock Who's There?*, the novel I'd been working on the summer before. The brothers who knew about the book were worried it would send Mummy right back to the bottle, and I certainly had my doubts. But it was part of the new me, the woman who decided that going forward, she would be telling the truth, no matter the risks.

I sent Mummy the first published copy with a note that read, "I started writing this book out of anger, but ended it with understanding."

She felt betrayed, and I didn't blame her. After all, the previous summer she'd made sure my kids were cared for on the beach while I wrote this novel, the thinly disguised story of living with an alcoholic mother. I wrote about her drunken behavior in the morning and ate dinner with her in the evening.

She wrote me a letter she never sent but took to her AA meeting to read aloud instead, her hands trembling with rage. At the end of the meeting, somebody asked her where I lived.

"In New York."

The man smiled. "I thought you might say Hong Kong or Fiji. Why don't you go see your daughter instead of writing to her?"

When Mummy called to tell me she was coming to New York to meet with me, I panicked. She hated the city, and I'd assumed, just as she had, that we were going, as usual, to duck any face-to-face confrontations and communicate our feelings about the book through letters or at the most, on the phone. It seems I wasn't the only one who'd decided to start facing the truth and talking about it.

I arranged for us to meet in my editor's apartment, as neither one of us were pretending that she was going to have dinner with the family or spend an afternoon in the playground with her grandchildren. This meeting had only one purpose, and when it was over, she would get back on the train and go home.

We sat together for four hours, longer than we'd ever spent in the same room, on the same topic of conversation, particularly one this explosive. I remember only bits and pieces of what we said.

"You exposed me. That was cruel."

"Mummy, anybody who knows my pseudonym knows you were an alcoholic."

She thought about that statement and acknowledged it with a nod. "I suppose that's true. Part of the disease is thinking you're getting away with it, that nobody is noticing."

Later in the day, she said, "I understand why you had to write the book, but why did you have to publish it?"

I didn't answer, and a few minutes later, she shrugged. "Of course, I understand. I was married to a writer."

She told me the ways in which she felt ignored by my father, her desperate shyness when she first arrived in America, pregnant at eighteen, how the fast social pace of life in post-war Washington had made her feel inadequate and overwhelmed. I listened.

At one point, I suggested that Daddy was also an alcoholic, but she bristled at that suggestion. "He drank heavily, but he wasn't an alcoholic." It seemed that she wanted to claim this disease as her own, stand alone in the spotlight for once, even as a drunk. I dropped the subject.

We both cried at different points during that day together, and at other times we laughed, and hugged one another once. And when the apartment began to grow dark and we were gathering our things together, I asked if she'd said all she came to say.

"I think so," she said, "but I'm too tired to really know."

"I know people will criticize me for writing the book," I said, "but I don't care what other people think. At least you and I have talked it through."

"No more secrets," she said to me hours later on the phone. "Let's not let anything come between us again."

☙

Slowly, we began to try to trust one another. At one point, when I decided to leave the children with her so I could meet their father in London, I arrived in Washington to find she'd hired a babysitter who only spoke Spanish.

"I thought you'd be here with them," I said the night I arrived.

"But I can't possibly do that, darling. I have a job now." She was working as a full-time volunteer at the Red Cross, training as a medical technologist.

"I thought you'd take the time off."

"Natalia will be very good with the children, I'm sure."

"She doesn't speak English, Mummy. And you've never seen her with children."

"She comes highly recommended. Andrew won't know the difference." He was eighteen months old.

"Eliza will," I said. I tried to make other arrangements, but it was too late. I was leaving the following evening.

The children survived. I created a calendar for Eliza, who crossed off each day I was gone before she went to sleep. Raymond, who had practically become my sixth brother, came up the street after school to play with the two of them. How foolish it was of me to think my mother would have handled it any other way. At last, her time was her own. She was sober, and my youngest brothers were both out of the house. Having spent so much of her life taking care of other people, she was determined to live every single day doing exactly what she wanted. And happy as she was to have her grandchildren visit because it meant I trusted that her sobriety would hold, her offer didn't include taking care of them herself.

And her sobriety did hold. Following a two-year course in medical technology and her training period, she was hired by the Red Cross in their biomedical research lab. For fifteen years, she went to work every day, stared through a microscope, and gave papers on blood rejection and purification at conferences as far away as Toronto. Although most of the old friends from her married days dropped her, she made new ones through work and her volunteer jobs with hospice and her church. For the first time since the war years at MI5 in London, she was a full-time working woman and proud of it. And she was genuinely happy.

Tish in 1995

Meanwhile, my marriage with Peter was coming apart. She and I talked often on the phone, so she knew what was happening to me. When I finally sued for divorce, she expressed outrage at the way I was being treated, both by my spouse and by the New York court system. She sent money before I even asked, and for the first few days of the trial, she sat in the courtroom beside my brother Joe. They'd both flown in to support me. And she was always there at the other end of the phone, prepared to listen and sympathize and offer help. Unhappy as I was, I loved being able to count on her. Those were our best years.

During those child-rearing years, my brothers and I were spread around the world, from California to Texas to Nepal. We kept in touch sporadically, while we married and raised children and worked, only rarely meeting all together. In 1994, at my mother's instigation, we had a reunion in Washington. In the photographs, the teenagers bond, my daughter—the eldest of the next generation—holds the youngest baby, and they all flank my mother, seated in a chair, holding court in her regal way.

It was only when our mother began to visibly age and lose her memory that we came together again. I took the lead, but they had my back. No longer huddled in the basement, we were still a tribe, this time working with one another to get through this next stage.

THE DARKNESS CLOSES IN

My mother's doctor calls to tell me what a nice quality of life my mother has. I believe she's trying to compliment me on the systems of care I've set up in the house, but I'm moved to write her a letter, detailing my mother's daily life.

Dear Dr. S,
You mention that my mother has such nice quality of life.
You are right in that we've kept her at home in her elegant and beloved house. She has full-time, live-in help. She has a sunny garden room and a bright and well-appointed bedroom. She's very lucky and we know it, but here's her real "quality of life."

As you and I have discussed, she will not complain to you and always insists that she is fine, has no pain, has no problems. But that is not the case, which I know from the daily caregivers and from my own time with her.

Her back has been so twisted by the spinal stenosis, the scoliosis, and arthritis that she can barely walk and only with crutches. She is often in pain.

She cannot taste or smell, so has not been able to enjoy food now for almost eight years, a particular torture for a woman whose two hobbies were cooking and gardening.

She cannot drive.

She cannot play bridge anymore.

She cannot track anything on television and often can't figure out how to turn the TV on or off.

She has very few visitors and when she does, she usually doesn't know who they are, where they came from and why they are there. She's not sure what to say to them and is scared she's repeating herself, so often lapses into silence.

She no longer wants to go to church.

When someone telephones her, she usually doesn't know who she's talking to.

She remembers none of her grandchildren specifically and is beginning to get her sons confused on the phone.

She can no longer read newspapers, books, anything because letters are a muddle to her, and she can't remember the beginning of the sentence by the time she gets to the end.

She can't listen to stories because she loses track of the thread in the middle.

Music agitates her.

The sun in her eyes agitates her. Sometimes even the small track lights in the ceiling agitate her.

She is always cold or complains of being so.

She is bored with her garden, sick of looking at it no matter how many birds and squirrels come and go.

She is almost incontinent.

It seems now that her one remaining pleasure comes when somebody, anybody takes her out for a drive in the car.

So please tell me, how do you define quality of life and what leads you to the conclusion that hers is "good?"

It's one of those letters I write but decide not to send. I am railing not so much at the doctor as at the dementia which has stolen my mother's mind from me before her body gave up. Because we missed so many years when I was growing up, I feel doubly robbed now.

The licensed practical nurses come and go. Two women now attend to my mother's every need and want. For a little while, Mummy seems happier, more lively, more engaged. Zuni and the nurses divide up their territories, and Zuni is thrilled with the medical backup and the company. The money flowing out just for the staff from the nursing agency is astounding, as high as $4,000 a week on top of the usual costs of maintaining the house and paying Zuni, Andrea, and Jan.

Then she grows more difficult. She won't let anybody in the

bathroom with her, but finally agrees to allow Sia, the day nurse, to watch her from the doorway when she takes a shower. Even so, she usually starts off the morning by yelling at Sia and Zuni.

"Get the hell out of my room. All of you."

When I visit, I try to have a serious talk with her.

"You know I've brought in extra nursing help for a reason, Mummy."

"I don't really need them."

"I'm hoping to keep you out of a nursing home."

"Well, dear, I want to stay here in my house."

"I know that. But if you don't let the nurse help you, then you could fall and then we'd have to take you to a nursing home."

"I do let them help."

"Yesterday, you told Sia to get the hell out of your room."

"Did I? It's because I don't like her watching me. I'm perfectly capable of taking a shower by myself."

"We don't want you to fall in the bathroom. Do you know that you have a fungal infection on your buttocks?"

"Well, no." Her chin is still lifted, but her voice falters just a bit.

"That's because it's harder for you to wash everywhere." I'm not enjoying this. Neither one of us is. "That's why you have to let Sia help you in the shower."

"All right, then, if you say so." Belligerent silence.

I've said it. It won't stick, I know, but at least I've tried.

And then she falls.

Zuni is standing at the open door of the bathroom when my mother suddenly crumples to the floor with no warning. Although she allows the ambulance drivers to lift her onto the bed, she yells at them that she won't go in the ambulance, and they back away, saying they don't have to make her. It's the Alzheimer's speaking, but, as usual, her voice is so determined and forceful that everybody around her gives in.

Although the mobile x-ray machine that comes to the house shows she has a fractured pelvis, nothing is displaced, so bed rest and pain medications are the only recommended course of action. Joe and I try to figure out how to cut back on the twenty-four-hour nursing and whether we can get Medicare to pay for the outpatient physical therapist.

The registered nurse reports that Mummy told her Sia is the nicest friend she's ever had. When I tell Joe that, he says wryly, "Right, better than her children or anybody else." But I'm actually touched by this new "friendship." It means she's regressing and becoming more childlike. It means she feels able to let down her guard with this sweet, smart woman from Sierra Leone in a way she never could with us or her husband or even her friends, except when she was drinking. That British stiff upper lip is softening. It also means that she's desperate to trust that someone will take care of her as the darkness closes in. And of course, it's Sia who's there every day by her side.

This is why the thought of moving her to a facility gives me such a pit in my stomach. She would lose her familiar surroundings, but also the first person she's ever trusted in her life. I honestly don't mind that it's not me. I'm relieved.

But things go downhill as we expected. When the doctor finally agrees that she needs to be admitted to the hospital, they find she has two major infections, a broken heel bone that the mobile x-ray hadn't picked up and a pool of liquid in the lower lobe of her left lung, because she has begun to aspirate fluids. All of this—combined with the fractured pelvis, the aortic stenosis, and the advanced dementia—means we no longer have a choice. She can't stay home anymore.

My heart is breaking. I go back to the medical directives that we first created together more than ten years ago, when she'd been taking care of a couple of elderly people in her church. She became their health proxies and faced tough decisions that she knew one day I might have to make for her. During a long weekend, when she was in her early seventies and fully cognizant, we talked about all sorts of end-of-life decisions. She didn't want any tubes, and she didn't want to be hydrated because she had to make that decision for a friend in London once and it did nothing but prolong her life needlessly. Finally, she wrote in a personal statement: "I would like to stay home, but if it is too difficult, then Elizabeth can decide."

My brother Ian and I are on rotation when we move her, on my sixty-fourth birthday, from the hospital to a private nursing home in nearby Maryland, where she can have her own room and the staff seems friendly and attentive. The head nurse on her floor is British, and I convince myself that the familiar accent will make my mother feel more at home. Zuni and Andrea spend most of the day with her, and we bring in an aide from four to eight in the evening, so she has almost no solitary time. Since each member of the nursing home staff is responsible for six patients, I know that without this extra help, there might be times when she is lying in bed calling for someone, and I can't stand the thought. As the dementia has advanced, she's become more and more frightened of being alone.

Ian and I meet with the new doctor, and together we go over the end-of-life directive. She makes sure we understand what no hydration means. We do. We tell her that we don't want our mother to go back to the hospital for any reason, and when the time comes, we want palliative care and hospice. We are all on the same page.

The first Sunday Mummy is in the nursing home, Ian decides we should bring in some familiar piece of art from her bedroom so she will feel comforted in this strange new place. I am hesitant, fearful this will backfire. She may have dementia, but she knows perfectly well she's not at home anymore. We choose an oil painting of Anne of Cleves from above the dressing table, the picture she used to see when she first opened her eyes to the eastern light that flooded her bedroom. The gilded frame looks ridiculously out of place in the pale green room with beige curtains, a hospital bed, and a utilitarian dresser.

The minute our mother sees the painting, she flies into a fury.

"Why have you brought that here?" she demands. "I'm not staying here, I'm going home."

We slink away to park the art in the head nurse's office until we can put it back in the car. "The first week is always the hardest," the British nurse assures us. "It will get better."

Although I continue to take comfort in her lovely Yorkshire accent, I doubt my mother will ever get used to this, will ever forgive me for taking her to this strange place. My mother was a founding member of the hospice movement in the United States, so naturally, I consider moving her home again. But I know that hospice must be ordered by a doctor and although the program assigns a team to the case, they only respond to requests for help from the staff in the house, which means we'd have to go back to full-time nursing.

I can't face the upheaval and will probably feel guilty about it forever.

Deep down I'm relieved that she is in a medical facility with a doctor on call who understands what we want and what we don't.

She is doing physical therapy covered by Medicare, but we don't think much progress is possible.

She has no quality of life. She stares vacantly out the window and, in the mornings, is agitated and angry. As the nurse explains, it's as if she is waking up every ten minutes in the middle of a movie. She doesn't know where she is, why she's there, when she's going home. She is still essentially Mummy. Distrustful, angry, petulant, imperious, dismissive, often amused. The food is crap. The PT is crap. But she knows she's not at home, and she wants to get back there no matter what.

"When will I be going home?" she asks again and again.

I've learned to say, "Well, Mummy, I think it's a matter of weeks, not days. And if you weren't here, you'd have to be in a hospital." That's the only thing that calms her down.

At one point, when Zuni and I are trying to help her find a

comfortable position and she's shaking with pain, she cries out, "What's happened to me?" That breaks my heart. She remembers nothing—not the pelvic fracture or the bedsore or the aortic stenosis or even the pain she experienced a few minutes ago. Nothing registers for longer than thirty seconds.

So, for us children, it's like living with an alcoholic again. When will she turn on us, explode, and then in the next minute laugh at a joke? How do we reach her? By telling her stories and showing her pictures and reminding her of her history—over and over again, because each time it's new.

There are funny moments too.

One afternoon, she asks me to read her list of medications.

"What's that pill for?" she demands, pointing at one in the paper cup.

"It's a memory booster."

"Well, that's certainly not working," she announces, and we both laugh.

Oddly enough, when she lost her sense of smell and taste, her hearing became even more acute and sensitive, although she can't always identify the sound. One morning, when an ambulance screams up the driveway outside her window, she frowns at me. "What is that ghastly noise?"

"An ambulance, Mummy."

"Well," she pronounces in her definitive voice, "at least it's not for me."

Zuni and Andrea attend to her every day. Andrea reports that Mummy cries sometimes. I think that's good because with her children, there's still the "no point fussing" attitude. She can't let her guard down with us. She never could with anybody but servants whom she can control and dismiss. And speaking Spanish comforts her.

Jan will visit a couple of times a week. The grandchildren are sending cards. But hours hang so heavy on her hands.

Please, God, let her go. It's time.

The End and Afterward

Ten days after I finish the first draft of this book, my mother dies. She does not go as peacefully as I would have wished.

I comfort myself now with the knowledge that we must labor out of life the way we labor into this world, and the agitation my brother Joe witnesses that last morning is her version of that work. The hardest thing that happens to all of us, I believe, is to face the loss of control. She had been forced to let go, bit by bit, for the last four years, but until those final hours she still fought to hold on, still raged against the dying of the light. There did come, at the very end, a relaxation, a final breath and then silence.

As soon as I get word that the end is near, my husband and I head to Washington, but we don't make it. We are speeding down Interstate 95 somewhere between Wilmington and Baltimore when my brother texts me that she's stopped breathing. He tells me later that she said very clearly, "Jesus Christ, please take me," and then a few minutes afterward, "I'm following behind you." And then she was gone.

When we arrive at the nursing home, an aide from Ghana with a gold cross around her neck hugs me in the hallway.

"Your mother kept begging Jesus to take her," she whispers in my ear.

I pull away so she can see my smile. "Begged or ordered?" I ask, and that makes her smile in return.

Zuni, Andrea, and my sister-in-law are sitting in the room when I get there.

"I have a feeling she's been waiting for you to come," Christiane says to me as they file out of the room so I can be alone with my mother's body.

&

For the first week without her, while the six of us children organize a funeral service and then a burial next to my father in the Alsop plot in Connecticut, my failure to get to her bedside before she died haunts me. I have the grandiose notion that because she didn't see my face in those last moments, she felt totally abandoned. Later the hospice nurse, who was shocked herself at how quickly my mother had gone, suggests that what probably killed her was a blood clot that traveled to her heart. This often happens, she explains, with elderly patients who have been in bed for a long time. And my mother had a history of blood clots.

During my long letting go, a friend who'd been through this process herself says, "Remember, no guilt. You did all you could." But I'm not sure I truly did everything possible, and I don't think I ever will be.

I didn't visit as often as I could have. I stayed away from the uglier sights as her organs, from skin to intestines, gave way. I told myself I was preserving her dignity. She could accept intimate attentions from caregivers on the payroll or nurses she didn't know better than from her own daughter. She wouldn't want me, of all people, to see her that way. But I don't know if I'm just making up excuses, hiding behind the wall that our financial resources and her reserve erected between us. Perhaps she did feel I abandoned her. Perhaps she wanted me there but couldn't bring herself to ask. She might have grown used to my touch after a while. Maybe I should have tried to break through to that dark closed space inside her that nobody ever managed to open. Is that a daughter's job? I don't know.

In the years I was working on this book, I videotaped two interviews with her, one about her childhood in Gibraltar and the other on her time in London during the war. Up until days before she died, my mother still repeated details of her story. When my brothers and I visited her in the nursing home, in lieu of futile attempts at conversation, we showed her those videotapes, and read her the wartime letters Daddy had written

to his parents about her. They gave her great pleasure and often elicited a repeat of one little moment or another. "Yes, I
remember I wore a black dress that night at the Ritz," or "The
V-1 fell into Green Park across the street, thank God."

Remembering these moments gives me more peace than the
caretaking I did, the bills I handled, the nurses I hired, or the
daily phone calls. I took the time to make sure that her story, in
all its particular detail, was told.

ॐ

I had my first dream about Mummy a month after she died.
When I walked into the hospital, there she was—small, silver-haired, curled into her bed like a baby in fetal position. *Oh
no*, I thought, *she's still alive. I have to start taking care of her again.*
Then suddenly, my younger, efficient mother appeared, the
woman who'd survived the war, crossed the North Atlantic,
and who later worked for the Red Cross. She moved in front of
me to comfort the dying, elderly "baby" in the hospital bed. I
woke up with a huge sense of relief. I'm not in charge anymore.
I'm no longer the mother to my mother.

ॐ

And just when I thought this book was finished, my mother
sent me the equivalent of a postcard from the grave.

My brothers and I put her house up for sale in early spring,
which is the best time to show real estate in Washington because the city is exploding with azalea blossoms and the summer humidity is still to come. It sold quickly, which meant we
only had a short time to do the final clearing out.

I thought that in all the years I'd been working on my
mother's history, I'd found just about everything that house
held. I was wrong. We unearthed newspapers from the three
days after Lincoln was assassinated, orations on the death of
George Washington, a letter from Theodore Roosevelt to his
sister Corinne (our great-grandmother), a Whistler etching, di-
aries from the 1850s, four boxes of silver items (many of them
monogrammed with ancestors' initials), eleven miniatures of

people ranging from a Civil War general to a coquettish Spanish dancer eyeing the viewer over her bare shoulder. What a bunch of pack rats our family turned out to be.

But for me, the most remarkable document in the entire house was the original copy of a speech my mother gave to a hospice group in 1984 about the grieving process she went through when my father, her husband of thirty years, died at sixty, leaving her a widow at the age of forty-eight. This, along with the notes she made for it, surfaced in a folder marked simply, PHA MEMORABILIA. Here is a shortened version of the speech which I've combined with her prep notes. The underlines are all hers.

I was born and brought up in Gibraltar. My father was a conventional Tory Englishman, a fair businessman but passionate about sports of all kinds, and very good at them. My mother was the product of a more exotic background; Italian, Spanish, Irish, and English. She was emotional, outgoing, childlike, charming—they were an unlikely couple. I went to England to boarding school in 1939—and grew up in wartime with all the restrictions and uncertainties that that entailed.

Stew and I met at a weekend party in the north of England. It was a farewell party for the owners as the house was taken over by the RAF. He was twenty-eight, an American and in the British Army—I was sixteen and just out of school.

We were married two years later in London during an air raid and after quite a number of separations and reunions, found ourselves in Washington in January of 1945. Traditional marriage. "Whither thou goest…" very literally since I crossed the ocean. I was very much Mrs. Stewart Alsop, and more so as his career blossomed and his reputation as a political journalist grew. For twenty-seven years I was the baby among our ever-enlarging group of friends—partly because of our age difference and partly because of Stew's work they came from the upper levels of government, the people he interviewed and saw every day. It was not a life

I had any experience with; a great deal of entertaining and masses of politics. The first dinner party I gave, I sat between the French Ambassador and a Supreme Court Justice and I was nineteen.

In July 1971, Stew was told he had leukemia. Very gradually over the next two years and ten months, our roles changed. He needed tremendous support and reassurance, and I was able to provide it, although it always had to be in the background. The first wave of loss came over me the first night I left Stew in the hospital at N.I.H. I sat in the car and cried. I don't know how long it was before I was able to start it and drive home. After that the sense of loss faded as my life changed and became totally focused on Stew; his blood counts, his infections and particularly all the support systems to be set up to enable him to live his life as normally as possible. For the first year and a half this was pretty normal. After that, the time he spent in the hospital mounted up until the last four months were almost entirely as an in-patient. I came back from supper one evening to find he had slipped away from me, and could barely speak, too late to say goodbye—he had the beginnings of a massive stroke. I felt cheated that I hadn't been able to say goodbye—even after almost three years of illness where death was the only result. He was in a coma for a week, a terrible time, when grief was overwhelming, but mourning seemed inappropriate. I was a widow in reality, but not in fact, and I felt totally unbalanced. I think my children felt the same way, and we comforted each other, but in a blind groping fashion. Stew's death was a release and a relief. I was so tired.

She talks about the arguments she and my oldest brother, Joe, had with the undertaker about a plain pine coffin (such a thing doesn't exist, we learned when we chose hers), and the words for the service.

Stew had very strong feelings about the language of the Bible, only the King James version. Elizabeth typed the funeral service word for word so that the minister would not make a mistake. The clothes I gave the undertaker to bury Stew in had not been cleaned—this was not disrespectful. Stew had never paid an enormous amount of attention to his appearance—he said that both his brothers were dandies and he would leave it up to them. We buried him in Middletown, Connecticut next to his parents and came home.

For two years the younger children and myself lived a life as close to the old life as possible. I felt I owed it to them. I had had to neglect them during Stew's illness—it was either the children or him. I don't think I was any help to my older children—in fact I know I was a burden.

Those two years were spent grieving, in denial and attempts at escape. (This is her only reference to the drinking, and she doesn't choose to elaborate.) I didn't start mourning Stew until my mother died two and a half years after his death. I went to her funeral in England in January of 1977, came home and fell apart. (This was the first explanation I ever heard for that month in her bedroom, the time that ended in a straitjacket.) It took me about a month to fall apart. I felt like a large jigsaw puzzle that had been dumped on the floor just after I had finished the edges. It was devastating. I felt alienated, abandoned, incompetent, emotionally out of control, and frightened. The major reason for my fear was that I thought I had "got over" Stew's death.

So I went away for a few weeks and started therapy. It took a while for me to learn that I couldn't shortchange the process of mourning, that I needed to face all the ambivalent feelings I had about Stew, our life together, his death and to develop my own sense of value about myself. I came to terms with my guilt at being alive and Stew dead, with my anger at him for dying and leaving me with all the problems of bringing up and looking after six children, leaving me with the loneliness and uncertainty of "who will look after me?", leaving me with the empty void after thirty years of marriage. It took me two years to feel confident enough to leave therapy.

I learned that my need for support, comforting consolation,

love, and acceptance for myself were not strange, but just plain human. I learned that it is all right to ask for help, for understanding from family, friends, and sometimes from strangers—it has never been refused. I find it much easier to console, now that I have been consoled, to comfort now that I have learned to accept comfort. It may be possible for saints always to give, but for me as an ordinary human being, it is far more effective as a two-way street.

I have been a widow for nine years and ten months and it has been a rocky road. What I have learnt primarily is to be honest with myself—if I am lonely, I reach out. If I am depressed—reach out. If I am tired—rest. Listen to myself—I am not the only friend I have, but I am certainly the closest.

So here I am. I have a job I love (medical research technologist with the Red Cross), with people I like and respect. My varied children appear to be thriving and their children. I have many old friends, who I don't see as often as when Stew was living and many new friends. Stew would say that I have no social life, and in his eyes I probably don't, but I have what I want and if I want more, I will go get it. I still live in the house Stew and I shared for twenty-three years. It is now my house, though it took several years for it to become mine.

I am a survivor and proud of it—I hope what I have said may help some of you—BUT I DO WANT you to know that it has helped me tremendously to talk to you today.

When I started writing this story, I made two arrogant assumptions. First, that although my mother was a wonderful storyteller, she wasn't really a writer. And secondly, that she hadn't lived what we call "an examined life." I was wrong on both counts. Although she wrote the speech for delivery, not publication, both the early notes and the final version reveal a person who not only knew herself, but who could communicate her innermost feelings, both negative and positive, with clarity and startling honesty. Just the way my father wrote her the equivalent of a love letter on the back page of *Newsweek* soon after he was diagnosed with incurable leukemia, she told a roomful of strangers about the inner emotional road she traveled from teenage war bride to survivor widow. She just didn't choose to share those feelings with me or anybody else in the family, as far as I know.

If I've learned anything from writing this book, it's that I don't know much. Do any of us?

Theirs was a wildly romantic beginning, but by the time I came along, the marriage had crashed into the reality of post-war life in Washington. My father traveled as much as six months a year. My mother was often pregnant, or nursing, or getting over a miscarriage. She was lonely when he was away traveling. He was lonely when she disappeared into her bedroom with a bottle. The strains of constant entertaining while raising six children on a journalist's income were considerable. Between my mother's periodic withdrawals and my father's distant parenting style, it makes sense that I wanted to focus on their wartime courtship. But when I read her speech, I found the answer to the question I didn't quite know I was asking: that despite all the rough times in the thirty years between wartime romance and his death by cancer, they had always loved one another in the ways that matter most.

ACKNOWLEDGEMENTS

For a book that has taken this long to write, it's hard to know where to start when acknowledging the people who accompanied me on the journey. I hope to be forgiven for any I may have left out.

While my mother was still alive, my husband and I traveled to Gibraltar to research her family roots and to see for ourselves what it was like to live on the Rock as she affectionately called it. James Gaggero, the son of her best friend growing up, put us up at the Rock Hotel and in every way he could, helped us find and photograph her childhood homes. The book of photographs I gave her when I returned from that trip allowed her to relive her childhood in the last years of her life.

In England when I traveled in my mother's footsteps, I found many people who were willing and eager to help me experience her life through the places where she'd lived. I list them here in no particular order, but with deep gratitude to all of them for welcoming myself and my husband to my mother's native land and for allowing us to see the places she knew and loved.

Thanks to John, Margaret and Alexandra Barnard Hankey who invited us to lunch early in our trip and then met us again at Fetcham Park in Surrey where my grandfather spent his childhood. John was my mother's first cousin and a person she spoke of many times with affection. It was a thrill to meet him.

Christopher Wallace, the Kings Royal Rifle Corps historian, sent me invaluable information over the years about my uncle Ian Hankey's service in the Corps and the circumstances of his death in the Western Desert. Despite his illness, Christopher met us at the Green Jackets Museum in Winchester to give us a special, private tour and then insisted we visit Winchester Cathedral so that we could view the page in the Honor Roll listing the record of my uncle's death.

Verian, the owner of Whiteshoots Cottage Bed and Break-fast, introduced us to the current owners of my paternal great-grandmother's house in the village of Bourton on the Water. They kindly led me upstairs into what had been my mother's bedroom when she came to visit. I stood at the window, imagining her as a young girl and later a teenager who'd just learned of her brother's death, standing in the exact same spot, gazing out at the rolling hills of the Cotswolds.

Sandra and Malcolm Young, the owners of Fetcham Park in Surrey and Laura Caudery, their daughter, and the manager of the property, welcomed us into my grandfather's childhood home. They showed me the notation on the drawing room door of my grandfather's height at the age of twenty-four, inscribed one day in May of 1914, almost exactly a century before my own visit. I am also grateful to Vivien White, the local historian who wrote a short history of Fetcham Park and gave me many insights into the house and its past.

Edward and Nell Stourton graciously invited us to spend the night at their house, the Stables at Allerton Park, so that we could tour the castle up the hill where my parents first met and share memories and photographs of our entwined families.

Daniel Davison, welcomed us to the campus of Ample-forth College, my uncle Ian's boarding school in Yorkshire, and helped us find the places on the grounds that my uncle had photographed when he was a student there in the 1930s. Daniel also made sure that we attended Compline, the meditative evening service in the chapel, which brought me closer to the uncle I never had the chance to meet.

Angus McLeod is the Minister of St. Columba's Scottish Presbyterian Church on Pont Street in London directly across the street from the flat where my mother lived with her parents during the war. I gave him a rare photograph my uncle Ian had taken of the church the day after it was bombed during World War II.

Bets and Jane de la Pasture, cousins of my mother, welcomed us to their sheep farm on the border of Wales, a place my mother had stayed many a time.

I am especially indebted to Richard Crowder, the son of my mother's dear friend, Bee. He welcomed us twice to the island of Guernsey where Bee spent her last years so that she and my mother could see one another again when Bee was no longer able to travel. Those visits gave these two great friends time to reconnect after a long absence and more importantly, the opportunity to say goodbye.

In Washington, DC, I will be forever grateful to Jan, Zuni and Andrea who surrounded my mother in her final years. They made her feel safe and comfortable, and allowed me to care for her from a distance, knowing she was never left alone. I know from others what a tremendous gift their loving time and attention afforded me.

Every writer needs support. Here follows a list of my early readers, my stalwart champions, the cheering section that drowns out the tiny whispering voice inside that urges me to give up.

Frances Taliaferro, Margot Witty, Tav Holmes, Betsy Sachs, Minny Holland, Margaret Robinson, Virginia Corey, Jane Lunson, Jane Denitz Smith, and Margery Cuyler.

My brothers form the core of my tribe. Their loyalty and their presence, not only in person, but on the phone and over email, helped me feel less alone as we bore witness to our mother's physical and emotional decline. And because one can never have too many brothers, I have adopted two more, Raymond Rinn and Tim Gunn. I am grateful to them for their loving encouragement through the long process of writing this book.

A huge thanks goes to my children, Eliza and Andrew, who support me with their love, their strength, and their independence.

Finally, thank you to my husband, Jason, who accepts without complaint that a writer must disappear daily into a creative void. I always say that my journalist father had a sign on his door that read, "Please don't knock unless you're bleeding." With Jason, there is no need for a sign. I am deeply grateful to him for the way he loves and supports me by giving me the time and the room I need to write.